Towards a Poor Theatre

Towards a Poor Theatre contains texts by Jerzy Grotowski (1933-1999), interviews with him, and other supplementary material presenting his method and training. Originally published in 1968, it has established itself as a classic work on theatre.

Towards a Poor Theatre

Jerzy Grotowski

Edited by Eugenio Barba
Preface by Peter Brook

Routledge
A Theatre Arts Book
New York

A Theatre Arts Book, published by
Routledge
29 West 35th Street
New York, NY 10001
www.routledge-ny.com

First Routledge edition, 2002
By arrangement with Odin Teatret Forlag, Denmark
Routledge is an imprint of the Taylor & Francis Group.
Copyright © 1968 Jerzy Grotowski and Odin Teatret Forlag

Cataloging-in-Publication data is available from the Library of
Congress.

ISBN 0-87830-155-0

CONTENTS

Jerzy Grotowski created the Theatre Laboratory in 1959 in Opole, a town of 60,000 inhabitants in south-west Poland. Co-creator was his close collaborator, the well known literary and theatre critic, Ludwik Flaszen. In January 1965, the Theatre Laboratory moved to the university town of Wroclaw which, with its half a million inhabitants, is also the cultural capital of the Polish Eastern Territories. It was here that it attained its present status of Institute for Research into Acting. The activities of the Laboratory have been continually subsidized by the State through the municipalities of Opole and Wroclaw.

The name itself reveals the nature of the undertaking. It is not a theatre in the usual sense of the word, but rather an institute devoted to research into the domain of the theatrical art and the art of the actor in particular. The Theatre Laboratory's productions represent a kind of working model in which the current research into the actor's art can be put into practice. Within the theatre milieu, this is known as the method of Grotowski. In addition to its methodical research work and performances given before an audience, the Laboratory also undertakes the instruction of actors, producers and people from other fields connected with the theatre.

The Theatre Laboratory has its own permanent troupe whose members also function as instructors. Students, many of them foreigners, are also accepted on a short term basis. Close contact is maintained with specialists in other disciplines such as psychology, phonology, cultural anthropology, etc.

The Theatre Laboratory is coherent in its choice of repertoire. The plays performed are based on the great Polish and international classics whose function is close to the myth in the collective consciousness. The productions which testify to the progressive stages of Grotowski's methodical and artistic research are the following: Byron's **Cain,** Kalidasa's **Shakuntala,** Mickiewicz's **Forefathers' Eve,** Slowacki's **Kordian,** Wyspianski's **Akropolis,** Shakespeare's **Hamlet,** Marlowe's **Dr Faustus** and Calderon's **The Constant Prince** in the Polish transcription by Slowacki. At present a production is in preparation based on themes from the Gospel. The Theatre Laboratory also tours abroad giving performances. Jerzy Grotowski frequently visits various theatre centres in different countries, giving theoretical and practical courses in his method.

Grotowski's closest collaborator in this research is Ryszard Cieslak who, in the opinion of a critic from the French newspaper "l'Express", is the living image of this method in his role as the Constant Prince.

9

PREFACE

by Peter Brook

Grotowski is unique.

Why?

Because no-one else in the world, to my knowledge, no-one since Stanislavski, has investigated the nature of acting, its phenomenon, its meaning, the nature and science of its mental-physical-emotional processes as deeply and completely as Grotowski.

He calls his theatre a laboratory. It is. It is a centre of research. It is perhaps the only avant-garde theatre whose poverty is not a drawback, where shortage of money is not an excuse for inadequate means which automatically undermine the experiments. In Grotowski's theatre as in all true laboratories the experiments are scientifically valid because the essential conditions are observed. In his theatre, there is absolute concentration by a small group, and unlimited time. So if you are interested in his findings you must go to Poland.

Or else do what we did. Bring Grotowski here.

He worked for two weeks with our group. I won't describe the work. Why not? First of all, such work is only free if it is in confidence, and confidence depends on its confidences not being disclosed. Secondly, the work is essentially non-verbal. To verbalise is to complicate and even to destroy exercises that are clear and simple when indicated by a gesture and when executed by the mind and body as one.

What did the work do?

It gave each actor a series of shocks.

The shock of confronting himself in the face of simple irrefutable challenges.

The shock of catching sight of his own evasions, tricks and clichés.

The shock of sensing something of his own vast and untapped resources.

The shock of being forced to question why he is an actor at all.

The shock of being forced to recognise that such questions do exist and that – despite a long English tradition of avoiding seriousness in theatrical art – the time comes when they must be faced. And of finding that he wants to face them.

The shock of seeing that somewhere in the world acting is an art of absolute dedication, monastic and total. That Artaud's now-hackneyed phrase 'cruel to myself' is genuinely a complete way of life – somewhere – for less than a dozen people.

11

With a proviso. This dedication to acting does not make acting an end in itself. On the contrary. For Grotowski acting is a vehicle. How can I put it? The theatre is not an escape, a refuge. A way of life is a way to life. Does that sound like a religious slogan? It should do. And that's about all there was to it. No more, no less. Results? Unlikely. Are our actors better? Are they better men? Not in that way, as far as I can see, not as far as anyone has claimed. (And of course they were not all ecstatic about their experience. Some were bored.)

But as Arden says:

> For the apple holds a seed will grow,
> In live and lengthy joy
> To raise a flourishing tree of fruit,
> Forever and a day.

Grotowski's work and ours have parallels and points of contact. Through these, through sympathy, through respect, we came together.

But the life of our theatre is in every way different from his. He runs a laboratory. He needs an audience occasionally, in small numbers. His tradition is Catholic – or anti-Catholic; in this case the two extremes meet. He is creating a form of service. We work in another country, another language, another tradition. Our aim is not a new Mass, but a new Elizabethan relationship – linking the private and the public, the intimate and the crowded, the secret and the open, the vulgar and the magical. For this we need both a crowd on stage and a crowd watching – and within that crowded stage individuals offering their most intimate truths to individuals within that crowded audience, sharing a collective experience with them.

We have come quite a way in developing an overall pattern – the idea of a group, of an ensemble.

But our work is always too hurried, always too rough for the development of the collection of individuals out of whom it is composed.

We know in theory that every actor must put his art into question daily – like pianists, dancers, painters – and that if he doesn't he will almost certainly get

12

stuck, develop clichés, and eventually decline. We recognise this and yet can do so little about it that we endlessly chase after new blood, after youthful vitality – except for certain of the most gifted exceptions, who of course get all the best chances, absorb most of the available time.

The Stratford Studio was a recognition of this problem, but it continually ran up against the strain of a repertory, of an overworked company, of simple fatigue.

Grotowski's work was a reminder that what he achieves almost miraculously with a handful of actors is needed to the same extent by each individual in our two giant companies in two theatres 90 miles apart.

The intensity, the honesty and the precision of his work can only leave one thing behind. A challenge. But not for a fortnight, not for once in a lifetime. Daily.

Towards a Poor Theatre

This article by Jerzy Grotowski has been published in: **Odra** (Wroclaw, 9/1965); **Kungs Dramatiska Teaterns Program** (Stockholm, 1965); **Scena** (Novi Sad, 5/1965); **Cahiers Renaud-Barrault** (Paris, 55/1966); **Tulane Drama Review** (New Orleans, T 35, 1967). Translation: T. K. Wiewiorowski.

I am a bit impatient when asked, "What is the origin of your experimental theatre productions?" The assumption seems to be that "experimental" work is tangential (toying with some "new" technique each time) and tributary. The result is supposed to be a contribution to modern staging – scenography using current sculptural or electronic ideas, contemporary music, actors independently projecting clownish or cabaret stereotypes. I know that scene: I used to be part of it. Our Theatre Laboratory productions are going in another direction. In the first place, we are trying to avoid eclecticism, trying to resist thinking of theatre as a composite of disciplines. We are seeking to define what is distinctively theatre, what separates this activity from other categories of performance and spectacle. Secondly, our productions are detailed investigations of the actor-audience relationship. That is, **we consider the personal and scenic technique of the actor as the core of theatre art.**

It is difficult to locate the exact sources of this approach, but I can speak of its tradition. I was brought up on Stanislavski; his persistent study, his systematic renewal of the methods of observation, and his dialectical relationship to his own earlier work make him my personal ideal. Stanislavski asked the key methodological questions. Our solutions, however, differ widely from his – sometimes we reach opposite conclusions.

I have studied all the major actor-training methods of Europe and beyond. Most important for my purposes are: Dullin's rhythm exercises, Delsarte's investigations of extroversive and intro-versive reactions, Stanislawski's work on "physical actions", Meyerhold's bio-mechanical training, Vakhtanghov's synthesis. Also particularly stimulating to me are the training techniques of oriental theatre – specifically the Peking Opera, Indian Kathakali, and Japanese No theatre. I could cite other theatrical systems, but the method which we are developing is not a combination of techniques borrowed from these sources (although we sometimes adapt elements for our use). We do not want to teach the actor a predetermined set of skills or give him a "bag of tricks." Ours is not a deductive method of collecting skills. Here everything is concentrated on the "ripening" of the actor which is expressed by a tension towards the extreme, by a complete stripping down, by the laying bear of one's own intimity – all this without the least trace of egotism or self-enjoyment. The actor makes a total gift of himself. This is a technique of the "trance" and of the integration of all the actor's psychic and bodily powers which emerge from the most intimate layers of his being and his instinct, springing forth in a sort of "trans-lumination."

The education of an actor in our theatre is not a matter of teaching him something; we attempt to eliminate his organism's resistance to this psychic process. The result is freedom from the time-lapse between inner impulse and outer reaction in such a way that the impulse is already an outer reaction. Impulse and action are concurrent: the body vanishes, burns, and the spectator sees only a series of visible impulses.

16

Ours then is a **via negativa** – not a collection of skills but an eradication of blocks.

Years of work and of specially composed exercises (which, by means of physical, plastic and vocal training, attempt to guide the actor towards the right kind of concentration) sometimes permit the discovery of the beginning of this road. Then it is possible to carefully cultivate what has been awakened. The process itself, though to some extent dependent upon concentration, confidence, exposure, and almost disappearance into the acting craft, is not voluntary. The requisite state of mind is a passive readiness to realize an active role, a state in which one does not **"want to do that"** but rather **"resigns from not doing it."**

Most of the actors at the Theatre Laboratory are just beginning to work toward the possibility of making such a process visible. In their daily work they do not concentrate on the spiritual technique but on the composition of the role, on the construction of form, on the expression of signs – i.e., on artifice. There is no contradiction between inner technique and artifice (articulation of a role by signs). We believe that a personal process which is not supported and expressed by a formal articulation and disciplined structuring of the role is not a release and will collapse in shapelessness.

We find that artificial composition not only does not limit the spiritual but actually leads to it. (The tropistic tension between the inner process and the form strengthens both. The form is like a baited trap, to which the spiritual process responds spontaneously and against which it struggles.) The forms of common "natural" behavior obscure the truth; we compose a role as a system of signs which demonstrate what is behind the mask of common vision: the dialectics of human behavior. At a moment of psychic shock, a moment of terror, of mortal danger or tremendous joy, a man does not behave "naturally." A man in an elevated spiritual state uses rhythmically articulated signs, begins

17

to dance, to sing. A **sign,** not a common gesture, is the elementary integer of expression for us.

In terms of formal technique, we do not work by proliferation of signs, or by accumulation of signs (as in the formal repetitions of oriental theatre). Rather, we subtract, seeking **distillation** of signs by eliminating those elements of "natural" behavior which obscure pure impulse. Another technique which illuminates the hidden structure of signs is **contradiction** (between gesture and voice, voice and word, word and thought, will and action, etc.) – here, too, we take the **via negativa.**

It is difficult to say precisely what elements in our productions result from a consciously formulated program and what derive from the structure of our imagination. I am frequently asked whether certain "medieval" effects indicate an intentional return to "ritual roots." There is no single answer. At our present point of artistic awareness, the problem of mythic "roots," of the elementary human situation, has definite meaning. However, this is not a product of a "philosophy of art" but comes from the practical discovery and use of the rules of theatre. That is, the productions do not spring from **a priori** aesthetic postulates; rather, as Sartre has said: "Each technique leads to metaphysics."

For several years, I vacillated between practice-born impulses and the application of **a priori** principles, without seeing the contradiction. My friend and colleague Ludwik Flaszen was the first to point out this confusion in my work: the material and techniques which came spontaneously in preparing the production, from the very nature of the work, were revealing and promising; but what I had taken to be applications of theoretical assumptions were actually more functions of my personality than of my intellect. I realized that the production led to awareness rather than being the product of awareness. Since 1960, my emphasis has been on methodology. Through practical experimentation I sought to answer the questions with which I had begun: What is the theatre? What is unique about it? What can it do that film and television cannot? Two concrete conceptions crystallized: the poor theatre, and performance as an act of transgression.

By gradually eliminating whatever proved superfluous, we found that theatre can exist without make-up, without autonomic costume and scenography, without a separate performance area (stage), without lighting and sound effects, etc. It cannot exist without the actor-spectator relationship of perceptual, direct, "live" communion. This is an ancient theoretical truth, of course, but when rigorously tested in practice it undermines most of our usual ideas about theatre. It challenges the notion of theatre as a synthesis of disparate creative disciplines – literature, sculpture, painting, architecture, lighting, acting (under the direction of a **metteur-en-scene).** This "synthetic theatre" is the contemporary theatre, which we readily call the "Rich Theatre" – rich in flaws.

The Rich Theatre depends on artistic kleptomania, drawing from other disciplines, constructing hybrid-spectacles, conglomerates without backbone or integrity, yet presented as an organic artwork. By multiplying assimilated elements, the Rich Theatre tries to escape the impasse presented by movies and television. Since film and TV excel in the area of mechanical functions (montage, instantaneous change of place, etc.), the Rich Theatre countered with a blatantly compensatory call for "total theatre." The integration of borrowed mechanisms (movie screens onstage, for example) means a sophisticated technical plant, permitting great mobility and dynamism. And if the stage and/or auditorium were mobile, constantly changing perspective would be possible. This is all nonsense.

No matter how much theatre expands and exploits its mechanical resources, it will remain technologically inferior to film and television. Consequently, I propose poverty in theatre. We have resigned from the stage-and-auditorium plant: for each production, a new space is designed for the actors and spectators.

19

Thus, infinite variation of performer-audience relationships is possible. The actors can play among the spectators, directly contacting the audience and giving it a passive role in the drama (e.g. our productions of Byron's **Cain** and Kalidasa's **Shakuntala**). Or the actors may build structures among the spectators and thus include them in the architecture of action, subjecting them to a sense of the pressure and congestion and limitation of space (Wyspianski's **Akropolis**). Or the actors may play among the spectators and ignore them, looking through them. The spectators may be separated from the actors – for example, by a high fence, over which only their heads protrude **(The Constant Prince,** from Calderon); from this radically slanted perspective, they look down on the actors as if watching animals in a ring, or like medical students watching an operation (also, this detached, downward viewing gives the action a sense of moral trans-gression). Or the entire hall is used as a concrete place: Faustus' "last supper" in a monastery refectory, where Faustus entertains the spectators, who are guests at a baroque feast served on huge tables, offering episodes from his life. The elimination of stage-auditorium dichotomy is not the important thing – that simply creates a bare laboratory situation, an appropriate area for investigation. The essential concern is finding the proper spec-tator-actor relationship for each type of performance and embody-ing the decision in physical arrangements.

We forsook lighting effects, and this revealed a wide range of possibilities for the actor's use of stationary light-sources by deliberate work with shadows, bright spots, etc. It is particularly significant that once a spectator is placed in an illuminated zone, or in other words becomes visible, he too begins to play a part in the performance. It also became evident that the actors, like figures in El Greco's paintings, can "illuminate" through personal technique, becoming a source of "spiritual light."
We abandoned make-up, fake noses, pillow-stuffed bellies – everything that the actor puts on in the dressing room before performance. We found that it was consummately theatrical for

the actor to transform from type to type, character to character, silhouette to silhouette – while the audience watched – in a **poor** manner, using only his own body and craft. The composition of a fixed facial expression by using the actor's own muscles and inner impulses achieves the effect of a strikingly theatrical transubstantiation, while the mask prepared by a make-up artist is only a trick.

Like the Jeanette Stoner piece

Similarly, a costume with no autonomous value, existing only in connection with a particular character and his activities, can be transformed before the audience, contrasted with the actor's functions, etc. Elimination of plastic elements which have a life of their own (i.e., represent something independent of the actor's activities) led to the creation by the actor of the most elementary and obvious objects. By his controlled use of gesture the actor transforms the floor into a sea, a table into a confessional, a piece of iron into an animate partner, etc. Elimination of music (live or recorded) not produced by the actors enables the performance itself to become music through the orchestration of voices and clashing objects. We know that the text **per se** is not theatre, that it becomes theatre only through the actors' use of it – that is to say, thanks to intonations, to the association of sounds, to the musicality of the language.

Also like The Serpent @ ETW

(writing of Rivera, O'Hara, S.L. Parks)

The acceptance of poverty in theatre, stripped of all that is not essential to it, revealed to us not only the backbone of the medium, but also the deep riches which lie in the very nature of the art-form.

Why are we concerned with art? To cross our frontiers, exceed our limitations, fill our emptiness – fulfil ourselves. This is not a condition but a process in which what is dark in us slowly becomes transparent. In this struggle with one's own truth, this effort to peel off the life-mask, the theatre, with its full-fleshed perceptivity, has always seemed to me a place of provocation.

21

It is capable of challenging itself and its audience by violating accepted stereotypes of vision, feeling, and judgment – more jarring because it is imaged in the human organism's breath, body, and inner impulses. This defiance of taboo, this transgression, provides the shock which rips off the mask, enabling us to give ourselves nakedly to something which is impossible to define but which contains Eros and Caritas.

In my work as a producer, I have therefore been tempted to make use of archaic situations sanctified by tradition, situations (within the realms of religion and tradition) which are taboo. I felt a need to confront myself with these values. They fascinated me, filling me with a sense of interior restlessness, while at the same time I was obeying a temptation to blaspheme: I wanted to attack them, go beyond them, or rather confront them with my own experience which is itself determined by the collective experience of our time. This element of our productions has been variously called "collision with the roots," "the dialectics of mockery and apotheosis," or even "religion expressed through blasphemy; love speaking out through hate."

As soon as my practical awareness became conscious and when experiment led to a method, I was compelled to take a fresh look at the history of theatre in relation to other branches of knowledge, especially psychology and cultural anthropology. A rational review of the problem of myth was called for. Then I clearly saw that myth was both a primeval situation, and a complex model with an independent existence in the psychology of social groups, inspiring group behavior and tendencies.

The theatre, when it was still part of religion, was already theatre: it liberated the spiritual energy of the congregation or tribe by incorporating myth and profaning or rather transcending it. The spectator thus had a renewed awareness of his personal truth in the truth of the myth, and through fright and a sense of the sacred he came to catharsis. It was not by chance that the Middle Ages produced the idea of "sacral parody."

But today's situation is much different. As social groupings are less and less defined by religion, traditional mythic forms are in flux, disappearing and being reincarnated. The spectators are more and more individuated in their relation to the myth as corporate truth or group model, and belief is often a matter of intellectual conviction. This means that it is much more difficult to elicit the sort of shock needed to get at those psychic layers behind the life-mask. Group identification with myth – the equation of personal, individual truth with universal truth – is virtually impossible today.

What is possible? First, confrontation with myth rather than identification. In other words, while retaining our private experiences, we can attempt to incarnate myth, putting on its ill-fitting skin to perceive the relativity of our problems, their connection to the "roots," and the relativity of the "roots" in the light of today's experience. If the situation is brutal, if we strip ourselves and touch an extraordinarily intimate layer, exposing it, the life-mask cracks and falls away.

Secondly, even with the loss of a "common sky" of belief and the loss of impregnable boundaries, the perceptivity of the human organism remains. Only myth – incarnate in the fact of the actor, in his living organism – can function as a taboo. The violation of the living organism, the exposure carried to outrageous excess, returns us to a concrete mythical situation, an experience of common human truth.

Again, the rational sources of our terminology cannot be cited precisely. I am often asked about Artaud when I speak of "cruelty," although his formulations were based on different premises and took a different tack. Artaud was an extraordinary visionary, but his writings have little methodological meaning because they are not the product of long-term practical investigations. They are an astounding prophecy, not a program. When i speak of "roots" or "mythical soul," I am asked about Nietzsche; if I call it "group imagination," Durkheim comes up; if I call it "archetypes," Jung. But my formulations are not derived from humanistic disciplines, though I may use them for analysis. When I speak of the actor's expression of signs, I am asked about oriental theatre, particularly classical Chinese theatre (especially when it is known that I studied there). But the hieroglyphic signs of the oriental theatre are inflexible, like an alphabet, whereas the signs we use are the skeletal forms of human action, a crystallization of a role, an articulation of the particular psycho-physiology of the actor.

I do not claim that everything we do is entirely new. We are bound, consciously or unconsciously, to be influenced by the traditions, science and art, even by the superstitions and presentiments peculiar to the civilisation which has moulded us, just as we breathe the air of the particular continent which has given us life. All this influences our undertaking, though sometimes we may deny it. Even when we arrive at certain theoretic formulas and compare our ideas with those of our predecessors which I have already mentioned, we are forced to resort to certain retrospective corrections which themselves enable us to see more clearly the possibilities opened up before us.

When we confront the general tradition of the Great Reform of the theatre from Stanislavski to Dullin and from Meyerhold to Artaud, we realize that we have not started from scratch but are operating in a defined and special atmosphere. When our investigation reveals and confirms someone else's flash of intuition, we are filled with humility. We realize that theatre has certain objective laws and that fulfillment is possible only within them, or, as Thomas Mann said, through a kind of "higher obedience," to which we give our "dignified attention."

I hold a peculiar position of leadership in the Polish Theatre

Laboratory. I am not simply the director or producer or "spiritual instructor." In the first place, my relation to the work is certainly not one-way or didactic. If my suggestions are reflected in the spatial compositions of our architect Gurawski, it must be understood that my vision has been formed by years of collaboration with him.

There is something incomparably intimate and productive in the work with the actor entrusted to me. He must be attentive and confident and free, for our labor is to explore his possibilities to the utmost. His growth is attended by observation, astonishment, and desire to help; my growth is projected onto him, or, rather, is **found in him** – and our common growth becomes revelation. This is not instruction of a pupil but utter opening to another person, in which the phenomenon of "shared or double birth" becomes possible. The actor is reborn – not only as an actor but as a man – and with him, I am reborn. It is a clumsy way of expressing it, but what is achieved is a total acceptance of one human being by another.

The Theatre's New Testament

Eugenio Barba made this interview in 1964, adding the title **The Theatre's New Testament.** It was published in his book **Alla Ricerca del Teatro Perduto** (Marsilio Editore, Padova 1965) as well as in **Teatrets Teori og Teknikk** (Holstebro 1/1966) and **Théâtre et Université** (Nancy 5/1966). Translation: Jörgen Andersen and Judy Barba.

The very name "Theatre Laboratory" makes one think of scientific research. Is this an appropriate association?

The word research should not bring to mind scientific research. Nothing could be further from what we are doing than science **sensu stricto,** and not only because of our lack of qualifications, but also because of our lack of interest in that kind of work.

The word research implies that we approach our profession rather like the mediaeval wood carver who sought to recreate in his block of wood a form which already existed. We do not work in the same way as the artist or the scientist, but rather as the shoemaker looking for the right spot on the shoe in which to hammer the nail.

The other sense of the word research might seem a little irrational as it involves the idea of a penetration into human nature itself. In our age when all languages are confused as in the Tower of Babel, when all aesthetical genres intermingle, death threatens the theatre as film and television encroach upon its domain. This

27

makes us examine the nature of theatre, how it differs from the other art forms, and what it is that makes it irreplaceable.

Has your research led you to a definition?

What does the word theatre mean? This is a question we often come up against, and one to which there are many possible answers. To the academic, the theatre is a place where an actor recites a written text, illustrating it with a series of movements in order to make it more easily understood. Thus interpreted the theatre is a useful accessory to dramatic literature. The intellectual theatre is merely a variation of this conception. Its advocates consider it a kind of polemical tribune. Here too, the text is the most important element, and the theatre is there only to plug certain intellectual arguments, thus bringing about their reciprocal confrontation. It is a revival of the mediaeval art of the oratorical duel.

To the average theatre-goer, the theatre is first and foremost a place of entertainment. If he expects to encounter a frivolous Muse, the text does not interest him in the least. What attracts him are the so-called gags, the comic effects and perhaps the puns which lead back to the text. His attention will be directed mainly towards the actor as a centre of attraction. A young woman sufficiently briefly clad is in herself an attraction to certain theatre-goers who apply cultural criteria to her performance, though such a judgement is actually a compensation for personal frustration.

The theatre-goer who cherishes cultural aspirations likes from time to time to attend performances from the more serious repertoire, perhaps even a tragedy provided that it contains some melodramatic element. In this case his expectations will vary

28

widely. On the one hand he must show that he belongs to the best society where "Art" is a guarantee and, on the other, he wants to experience certain emotions which give him a sense of self-satisfaction. Even if he does feel pity for poor Antigone and aversion for the cruel Creon, he does not share the sacrifice and the fate of the heroine, but he nevertheless believes himself to be her equal morally. For him it is a question of being able to feel "noble". The didactic qualities of this kind of emotion are dubious. The audience – all Creons – may well side with Antigone throughout the performance, but this does not prevent each of them from behaving like Creon once out of the theatre. It is worth noticing the success of plays which depict an unhappy childhood. To see the sufferings of an innocent child on the stage makes it even easier for the spectator to sympathize with the unfortunate victim. Thus he is assured of his own high standard of moral values.

Theatre people themselves do not usually have an altogether clear conception of theatre. To the average actor the theatre is first and foremost **himself,** and not what he is able to achieve by means of his artistic technique. He – his own private organism – **is** the theatre. Such an attitude breeds the impudence and self-satisfaction which enable him to present acts that demand no special knowledge, that are banal and commonplace, such as walking, getting up, sitting down, lighting a cigarette, putting his hands in his pockets, and so on. In the actor's opinion all this is not meant to reveal anything but to be enough in itself for, as I said, he, the actor, Mr. X, **is** the theatre. And if the actor possesses a certain charm which can take in the audience, it strengthens him in his conviction.

To the stage-designer, the theatre is above all a plastic art and this can have positive consequences. Designers are often supporters of the literary theatre. They claim that the décor as well as the actor should serve the drama. This creed reveals no wish to serve literature, but merely a complex towards the producer. They prefer to be on the side of the playwright as he is further removed and consequently less able to restrict them. In practice, the most original stage-designers suggest a confrontation between the text and a plastic vision which surpasses and reveals the playwright's imagination. It is probably no mere coincidence that the Polish designers are often the pioneers in our country's theatre. They exploited the numerous possibilities offered by the revolutionary development of the plastic arts in the twentieth century which, to a lesser degree, inspired playwrights and producers.

Does this not imply a certain danger? The critics who accuse the designers of dominating the stage, put forward more than one valid objective argument, only their premise is erroneous. It is as if they blame a car for travelling faster than a snail. This is what worries them and not whether the designer's vision dominates that of the actor and the producer. The vision of the designer is creative, not stereotyped, and even if it is, it loses its tautological character through an immense magnification process. Nevertheless, the theatre is transformed – whether the designer likes it or not – into a series of living tableaux. It becomes a kind of monumental "camera oscura", a thrilling "laterna magica". But does it not then cease to be theatre?

Finally, what is the theatre to the producer? Producers come to the theatre after failing in other fields. He who once dreamed of becoming a playwright usually ends up as a producer.

The actor who is a failure, the actress who once played the young prima donna and is getting old, these turn to production.

The theatre critic who has long had an impotence complex towards an art which he can do no more than write about takes up producing.

30

The hypersensitive professor of literature who is weary of academic work considers himself competent to become a producer. He knows what drama is – and what else is theatre to him if not the realisation of a text?

Because they are guided by such varied psycho-analytic motives, producers' ideas on theatre are about as varied as it is possible to be. Their work is a compensation for various phenomena. A man who has unfulfilled political tendencies, for instance, often becomes a producer and enjoys the feeling of power such a position gives him. This has more than once led to perverse interpretations, and producers possessing such an extreme need for power have staged plays which polemize against the authorities: hence numerous "rebellious" performances.

Of course a producer wants to be creative. He therefore – more or less consciously – advocates an autonomous theatre, independent of literature which he merely considers as a pretext. But, on the other hand, people capable of such creative work are rare. Many are officially content with a literary and intellectual theatre definition, or to maintain Wagner's theory that the theatre should be a synthesis of all the arts. A very useful formula! It allows one to respect the text, that inviolable basic element, and furthermore it provokes no conflict with the literary and the philological milieu. It must be stated, in parenthesis, that every playwright – even the ones we can only qualify as such out of sheer politeness – feels himself obliged to defend the honour and the rights of Mickiewicz, Shakespeare, etc., because quite simply he considers himself their colleague. In this way Wagner's theory about "the theatre as the total art" establishes **la paix des braves** in the literary field.

This theory justifies the exploitation of the plastic elements of scenography in the performance, and ascribes the results to it. The same goes for the music, whether it be an original work or a montage. To this is added the accidental choice of one or more

31

well known actors and from these elements, only casually co-ordinated, emerges a performance which satisfies the ambitions of the producer. He is enthroned on top of all the arts, although in reality he feeds off them all without himself being tied to the creative work which is carried out for him by others – if, indeed, anyone can be called creative in such circumstances.

Thus the number of definitions of theatre is practically unlimited. To escape from this vicious circle one must without doubt eliminate, not add. That is, one must ask oneself what is indispensable to theatre. Let's see.

Can the theatre exist without costumes and sets? Yes, it can.

Can it exist without music to accompany the plot? Yes.

Can it exist without lighting effects? Of course.

And without a text? Yes; the history of the theatre confirms this. In the evolution of the theatrical art the text was one of the last elements to be added. If we place some people on a stage with a scenario they themselves have put together and let them improvise their parts as in the Commedia dell'Arte, the performance will be equally good even if the words are not articulated but simply muttered.

But can the theatre exist without actors? I know of no example of this. One could mention the puppet-show. Even here, however, an actor is to be found behind the scenes, although of another kind.

Can the theatre exist without an audience? At least one spectator is needed to make it a performance. So we are left with the actor and the spectator. We can thus define the theatre as "what takes place between spectator and actor". All the other things are supplementary – perhaps necessary, but nevertheless supplementary. It is no mere coincidence that our own theatre laboratory has developed from a theatre rich in resources – in which the plastic arts, lighting and music, were constantly exploited – into the ascetic theatre we have become in recent years: an ascetic theatre in which the actors and audience are all that is left. All the other visual elements – e. g. plastic, etc. – are constructed by means of the actor's body, the acoustic and musical effects by his voice. This does not mean that we look down upon literature, but that we do not find in it the creative part of the theatre, even though great literary works can, no doubt, have a stimulating effect on this genesis. Since our theatre consists only of actors and audience, we make special demands on both parties. Even though we cannot educate the audience – not systematically, at least – we **can** educate the actor.

How, then, is the actor trained in your theatre, and what is his function in the performance?

The actor is a man who works in public with his body, offering it publicly. If this body restricts itself to demonstrating what it is – something that any average person can do – then it is not an obedient instrument capable of performing a spiritual act. If it is exploited for money and to win the favour of the audience, then the art of acting borders on prostitution. It is a fact that for many centuries the theatre has been associated with prostitution in one sense of the word or another. The words "actress" and "courtesan" were once synonymous. Today they are separated by a somewhat clearer line, not through any change in the actor's world but because society has changed. Today it is the difference between the respectable woman and the courtesan which has become blurred.

What strikes one when looking at the work of an actor as practised these days is the wretchedness of it: the bargaining over a

33

body which is exploited by its protectors – director, producer – creating in return an atmosphere of intrigue and revolt.

Just as only a great sinner can become a saint according to the theologians (Let us not forget the Revelation: "So then because thou art lukewarm, and neither cold nor hot, I will spue thee out of my mouth"), in the same way the actor's wretchedness can be transformed into a kind of holiness. The history of the theatre has numerous examples of this.

Don't get me wrong. I speak about "holiness" as an unbeliever. I mean a "secular holiness". If the actor, by setting himself a challenge publicly challenges others, and through excess, profanation and outrageous sacrilege reveals himself by casting off his everyday mask, he makes it possible for the spectator to undertake a similar process of self-penetration. If he does not exhibit his body, but annihilates it, burns it, frees it from every resistance to any psychic impulse, then he does not sell his body but sacrifices it. He repeats the atonement; he is close to holiness. If such acting is not to be something transient and fortuitous, a phenomenon which cannot be foreseen in time or space: if we want a theatre group whose daily bread is this kind of work – then we must follow a special method of research and training.

What is it like, in practice, to work with the "holy" actor?
There is a myth telling how an actor with a considerable fund of experience can build up what we might call his own "arsenal" – i. e. an accumulation of methods, artifices and tricks. From these he can pick out a certain number of combinations for each part and thus attain the expressiveness necessary for him to grip his audience. This "arsenal" or store may be nothing but a collection of clichés, in which case such a method is inseparable from the conception of the "courtesan actor".

The difference between the "courtesan actor" and the "holy actor" is the same as the difference between the skill of a courtesan and the attitude of giving and receiving which springs from true love: in other words, self-sacrifice. The essential thing in this second case is to be able to eliminate any disturbing elements in order to be able to overstep every conceivable limit. In the first case it is a question of the existence of the body; in the other, rather of its non-existence. The technique of the "holy actor" is an **inductive technique** (i. e. a technique of elimination), whereas that of the "courtesan actor" is a **deductive technique** (i. e. an accumulation of skills).

The actor who undertakes an act of self-penetration, who reveals himself and sacrifices the innermost part of himself – the most painful, that which is not intended for the eyes of the world – must be able to manifest the least impulse. He must be able to express, through sound and movement, those impulses which waver on the borderline between dream and reality. In short, he must be able to construct his own psycho-analytic language of sounds and gestures in the same way that a great poet creates his own language of words.

If we take into consideration for instance the problem of sound, the plasticity of the actor's respiratory and vocal apparatus must be infinitely more developed than that of the man in the street. Furthermore, this apparatus must be able to produce sound reflexes so quickly that thought – which would remove all spontaneity – has no time to intervene.

The actor should be able to decipher all the problems of his body which are accessible to him. He should know how to direct the air to those parts of the body where sound can be created and amplified by a sort of resonator. The average actor knows only the head resonator; that is, he uses his head as a resonator to amplify his voice, making it sound more "noble", more agreeable to the audience. He may even at times, fortuitously, make use of the

35

chest resonator. But the actor who investigates closely the possibilities of his own organism discovers that the number of resonators is practically unlimited. He can exploit not only his head
and chest, but also the back of his head (occiput), his nose, his
teeth, his larynx, his belly, his spine, as well as a total resonator
which actually comprises the whole body and many others, some
of which are still unknown to us. He discovers that it is not enough
to make use of abdominal respiration on stage. The various phases
in his physical actions demand different kinds of respiration if he
is to avoid difficulties with his breathing and resistance from his
body. He discovers that the diction he learnt at drama school far
too often provokes the closing of the larynx. He must acquire the
ability to open his larynx consciously, and to check from the outside whether it is open or closed. If he does not solve these
problems, his attention will be distracted by the difficulties he is
bound to encounter and the process of self-penetration will
necessarily fail. If the actor is conscious of his body, he cannot
penetrate and reveal himself. The body must be freed from all
resistance. It must virtually cease to exist. As for his voice and
respiration, it is not enough that the actor learns to make use of
several resonators, to open his larynx and to select a certain type
of respiration. He must learn to perform all this unconsciously in
the culminating phases of his acting and this, in its turn, is something which demands a new series of exercises. When he is working on his role he must learn not to think of adding technical
elements (resonators, etc.), but should aim at eliminating the concrete obstacles he comes up against (e. g. resistance in his voice).

This is not merely splitting hairs. It is the difference which decides
the degree of success. It means that the actor will never possess
a permanently "closed" technique, for at each stage of his self-
scrutiny, each challenge, each **excess,** each breaking down of
hidden barriers he will encounter new technical problems on a
higher level. He must then learn to overcome these too with the
help of certain basic exercises.

This goes for everything: movement, the plasticity of the body, gesticulation, the construction of masks by means of the facial musculature and, in fact, for each detail of the actor's body.

But the decisive factor in this process is the actor's technique of psychic penetration. He must learn to use his role as if it were a surgeon's scalpel, to dissect himself. It is not a question of portraying himself under certain given circumstances, or of "living" a part; nor does it entail the distant sort of acting common to epic theatre and based on cold calculation. The important thing is to use the role as a trampolin, an instrument with which to study what is hidden behind our everyday mask – the innermost core of our personality – in order to sacrifice it, expose it.

This is an excess not only for the actor but also for the audience. The spectator understands, consciously or unconsciously, that such an act is an invitation to him to do the same thing, and this often arouses opposition or indignation, because our daily efforts are intended to hide the truth about ourselves not only from the world, but also from ourselves. We try to escape the truth about ourselves, whereas here we are invited to stop and take a closer look. We are afraid of being changed into pillars of salt if we turn around, like Lot's wife.

The performing of this act we are referring to – self-penetration, exposure – demands a mobilization of all the physical and spiritual forces of the actor who is in a state of idle readiness, a passive availability, which makes possible an active acting score.

One must resort to a metaphorical language to say that the decisive factor in this process is humility, a spiritual predisposition: not to **do** something, but to **refrain** from doing something, otherwise the excess becomes impudence instead of sacrifice. This means that the actor must act in a state of trance.

Trance, as I understand it, is the ability to concentrate in a particular theatrical way and can be attained with a minimum of good-will.

If I were to express all this in one sentence I would say that it is all a question of giving oneself. One must give oneself totally, in one's deepest intimacy, with confidence, as when one gives one-self in love. Here lies the key. Self-penetration, trance, **excess,** the formal discipline itself – all this can be realized, provided one has given oneself fully, humbly and without defense. This act culminates in a climax. It brings relief. None of the exercises in the various fields of the actor's training must be exercises in skill. They should develop a system of allusions which lead to the elusive and indescribable process of self-donation.

All this may sound strange and bring to mind some form of "quackery". If we are to stick to scientific formulas, we can say that it is a particular use of suggestion, aiming at an **ideoplastic** realization. Personally, I must admit that we do not shrink from using these "quack" formulas. Anything that has an unusual or magical ring stimulates the imagination of both actor and pro-ducer.

I believe one must develop a special anatomy of the actor; for instance, find the body's various centres of concentration for different ways of acting, seeking the areas of the body which the actor sometimes feels to be his sources of energy. The lumbar region, the abdomen and the area around the solar plexus often function as such a source.

An essential factor in this process is the elaboration of a guiding rein for the form, the artificiality. The actor who accomplishes an act of self-penetration is setting out on a journey which is recorded through various sound and gesture reflexes, formulating a sort of invitation to the spectator. But these signs must be articulated. Expressiveness is always connected with certain contradictions and discrepancies. Undisciplined self-penetration is no liberation, but is perceived as a form of biological chaos.

How do you combine spontaneity and formal discipline?

The elaboration of artificiality is a question of ideograms – sounds and gestures – which evoke associations in the psyche of the audience. It is reminiscent of a sculptor's work on a block of stone: the conscious use of hammer and chisel. It consists, for instance, in the analysis of a hand's reflex during a psychic process and its successive development through shoulder, elbow, wrist and fingers in order to decide how each phase of this process can be expressed through a sign, an ideogram, which either instantly conveys the hidden motivations of the actor or polemizes against them.

This elaboration of artificiality – of the form's guiding rein – is often based on a conscious searching of our organism for forms whose outlines we feel although their reality still escapes us. One assumes that these forms already exist, complete, within our organism. Here we touch on a type of acting which, as an art, is closer to sculpture than to painting. Painting involves the addition of colours, whereas the sculptor takes away what is concealing the form which, as it were, already exists within the block of stone, thus revealing it instead of building it up.

This search for artificiality in its turn requires a series of additional exercises, forming a miniature score for each part of the body. At any rate, the decisive principle remains the following: the more we become absorbed in what is hidden inside us, in the excess, in the exposure, in the self-penetration, the more rigid must be the external discipline; that is to say the form, the artificiality, the ideogram, the sign. Here lies the whole principle of expressiveness.

What do you expect from the spectator in this kind of theatre?

Our postulates are not new. We make the same demands on
people as every real work of art makes, whether it be a painting,
a sculpture, music, poetry or literature. We do not cater for the
man who goes to the theatre to satisfy a social need for contact
with culture: in other words, to have something to talk about to
his friends and to be able to say that he has seen this or that play
and that it was interesting. We are not there to satisfy his "cultural
needs". This is cheating.

Nor do we cater for the man who goes to the theatre to relax after
a hard day's work. Everyone has a right to relax after work and
there are numerous forms of entertainment for this purpose,
ranging from certain types of film to cabaret and music-hall, and
many more on the same lines.

We are concerned with the spectator who has genuine spiritual
needs and who really wishes, through confrontation with the performance, to analyse himself. We are concerned with the spectator
who does not stop at an elementary stage of psychic integration,
content with his own petty, geometrical, spiritual stability, knowing
exactly what is good and what is evil, and never in doubt. For it
was not to him that El Greco, Norwid, Thomas Mann and Dostoyev-
sky spoke, but to him who undergoes an endless process of self-
development, whose unrest is not general but directed towards a
search for the truth about himself and his mission in life.

Does this infer a theatre for the élite?

Yes, but for an élite which is not determined by the social background or financial situation of the spectator, nor even education.
The worker who has never had any secondary education can
undergo this creative process of self-search, whereas the uni-

versity professor may be dead, permanently formed, moulded into the terrible rigidity of a corpse. This must be made clear from the very beginning. We are not concerned with just any audience, but a special one.

We cannot know whether the theatre is still necessary today since all social attractions, entertainments, form and colour effects have been taken over by film and television. Everybody repeats the same rhetorical question: is the theatre necessary? But we only ask it in order to be able to reply: yes, it is, because it is an art which is always young and always necessary. The sale of performances is organized on a grand scale. Yet no one organizes film and television audiences in the same way. If all theatres were closed down one day, a large percentage of the people would know nothing about it until weeks later, but if one were to eliminate cinemas and television, the very next day the whole population would be in an uproar. Many theatre people are conscious of this problem, but hit upon the wrong solution: since the cinema dominates theatre from a technical point of view, why not make the theatre more technical? They invent new stages, they put on performances with lightning-quick changes of scenery, complicated lighting and décor, etc., but can never attain the technical skill of film and television. The theatre must recognize its own limitations. If it cannot be richer than the cinema, then let it be poor. If it cannot be as lavish as television, let it be ascetic. If it cannot be a technical attraction, let it renounce all outward technique. Thus we are left with a "holy" actor in a poor theatre.

There is only one element of which film and television cannot rob the theatre: the closeness of the living organism. Because of this, each challenge from the actor, each of his magical acts (which the audience is incapable of reproducing) becomes something great, something extraordinary, something close to ecstacy. It is therefore necessary to abolish the distance between actor and audience by eliminating the stage, removing all frontiers. Let the most

41

drastic scenes happen face to face with the spectator so that he is within arm's reach of the actor, can feel his breathing and smell the perspiration. This implies the necessity for a chamber theatre.

How can such a theatre express the unrest which one has a right to assume varies with the individual?

In order that the spectator may be stimulated into self-analysis when confronted with the actor, there must be some common ground already existing in both of them, something they can either dismiss in one gesture or jointly worship. Therefore the theatre must attack what might be called the collective complexes of society, the core of the collective subconscious or perhaps super-conscious (it does not matter what we call it), the myths which are not an invention of the mind but are, so to speak, inherited through one's blood, religion, culture and climate.

I am thinking of things that are so elementary and so intimately associated that it would be difficult for us to submit them to a rational analysis. For instance, religious myths: the myth of Christ and Mary; biological myths: birth and death, love symbolism or, in a broader sense, Eros and Thanatos; national myths which it would be difficult to break down into formulas, yet whose very presence we feel in our blood when we read Part III of Mickie-wicz's "Forefathers' Eve", Slowacki's "Kordian" or the Ave Maria.

Once again, there is no question of a speculative search for certain elements to be assembled into a performance. If we start working on a theatre performance or a role by violating our inner-most selves, searching for the things which can hurt us most deeply, but which at the same time give us a total feeling of purifying truth that finally brings peace, then we will inevitably end up with **representations collectives.** One has to be familiar with this concept so as not to lose the right track once one has found it. But it cannot be imposed on one in advance.

How does this function in a theatre performance? I do not intend to give examples here. I think there is sufficient explanation in the description of "Akropolis", "Dr Faustus" or other performances. I only wish to draw attention to a special characteristic of these theatre performances which combine fascination and excessive negation, acceptation and rejection, an attack on that which is sacred **(representations collectives),** profanation and worship.

To spark off this particular process of provocation in the audience, one must break away from the trampolin represented by the text and which is already overloaded with a number of general associations. For this we need either a classical text to which, through a sort of profanation, we simultaneously restore its truth, or a modern text which might well be banal and stereotyped in its content, but nevertheless rooted in the psyche of society.

Is the "holy" actor not a dream? The road to holiness is not open to everyone. Only the chosen few can follow it.

As I said, one must not take the word "holy" in the religious sense. It is rather a metaphor defining a person who, through his art, climbs upon the stake and performs an act of self-sacrifice. Of course, you are right: it is an infinitely difficult task to assemble a troup of "holy" actors. It is very much easier to find a "holy" spectator – in my sense of the word – for he only comes to the theatre for a brief moment in order to square off an account with himself, and this is something that does not impose the hard routine of daily work.

Is holiness therefore an unreal postulate? I think it is just as well founded as that of movement at the speed of light. By this I mean that without ever attaining it, we can nevertheless move consciously and systematically in that direction, thus achieving practical results.

43

Acting is a particularly thankless art. It dies with the actor. Nothing survives him but the reviews which do not usually do him justice anyway, whether he is good or bad. So the only source of satisfaction left to him is the audience's reactions. In the poor theatre this does not mean flowers and interminable applause, but a special silence in which there is much fascination but also a lot of indignation, and even repugnance, which the spectator directs not at himself but at the theatre. It is difficult to reach a psychic level which enables one to endure such pressure.

I am sure that every actor belonging to such a theatre often dreams of overwhelming ovations, of hearing his name shouted out, of being covered with flowers or other such symbols of appreciation as is customary in the commercial theatre. The actor's work is also a thankless one because of the incessant supervision it is subject to. It is not like being creative in an office, seated before a table, but under the eye of the producer who, even in a theatre based on the art of the actor, must make persistent demands on him to a much greater extent than in the normal theatre, urging him on to ever increasing efforts that are painful to him.

This would be unbearable if such a producer did not possess a moral authority, if his postulates were not evident, and if an element of mutual confidence did not exist even beyond the barriers of consciousness. But even in this case, he is nevertheless a tyrant and the actor must direct against him certain unconscious mechanical reactions like a pupil does against his teacher, a patient against his doctor, or a soldier against his superiors.

The poor theatre does not offer the actor the possibility of overnight success. It defies the bourgeois concept of a standard of living. It proposes the substitution of material wealth by moral wealth as the principal aim in life. Yet who does not cherish a secret wish to rise to sudden affluence? This too may cause

44

opposition and negative reactions, even if these are not clearly formulated. Work in such an ensemble can never be stable. It is nothing but a huge challenge and, furthermore, it awakens such strong reactions of aversion that these often threaten the theatre's very existence. Who does not search for stability and security in one form or another? Who does not hope to live at least as well tomorrow as he does today? Even if one consciously accepts such a status, one unconsciously looks around for that unattainable refuge which reconciles fire with water and "holiness" with the life of the "courtesan".

However, the attraction of such a paradoxical situation is sufficiently strong to eliminate all the intrigues, slander and quarrels over roles which form part of everyday life in other theatres. But people will be people, and periods of depression and suppressed grudges cannot be avoided.

It is nevertheless worth mentioning that the satisfaction which such work gives is great. The actor who, in this special process of discipline and self-sacrifice, self-penetration and moulding, is not afraid to go beyond all normally acceptable limits, attains a kind of inner harmony and peace of mind. He literally becomes much sounder in mind and body, and his way of life is more normal than that of an actor in the rich theatre.

This process of analysis is a sort of disintegration of the psychic structure. Is the actor not in danger here of overstepping the mark from the point of view of mental hygiene?

No, provided that he gives himself one hundred per cent to his work. It is work that is done half-heartedly, superficially, that is psychically painful and upsets the equilibrium. If we only engage ourselves superficially in this process of analysis and exposure –

and this can produce ample aesthetical effects – that is, if we retain our daily mask of lies, then we witness a conflict between this mask and ourselves. But if this process is followed through to its extreme limit, we can in full consciousness put back our everyday mask, knowing now what purpose it serves and what it conceals beneath it. This is a confirmation not of the negative in us but of the positive, not of what is poorest but of what is richest. It also leads to a liberation from complexes in much the same way as psycho-analytic therapy.

The same also applies to the spectator. The member of an audience who accepts the actor's invitation and to a certain extent follows his example by activating himself in the same way, leaves the theatre in a state of greater inner harmony. But he who fights to keep his mask of lies intact at all costs, leaves the performance even more confused. I am convinced that on the whole, even in the latter case, the performance represents a form of social psycho-therapy, whereas for the actor it is only a therapy if he has given himself whole-heartedly to his task.

There are certain dangers. It is far less risky to be Mr. Smith all one's life than to be Van Gogh. But, fully conscious of our social responsibility, we could wish that there were more Van Goghs than Smiths, even though life is much simpler for the latter. Van Gogh is an example of an incomplete process of integration. His downfall is the expression of a development which was never fulfilled. If we take a look at great personalities like for example Thomas Mann, we do eventually find a certain form of harmony.

It seems to me that the producer has a very great responsibility in this self-analytic process of the actor. How does this interdependence manifest itself, and what might be the consequences of a wrong action on his part?

This is a vitally important point. In the light of what I have just said, this may sound rather strange.

The performance engages a sort of psychic conflict with the spectator. It is a challenge and an excess, but can only have any effect if based on human interest and, more than that, on a feeling of sympathy, a feeling of acceptation. In the same way, the producer can help the actor in this complex and agonizing process only if he is just as emotionally and warmly open to the actor as the actor is in regard to him. I do not believe in the possibility of achieving effects by means of cold calculation. A kind of warmth towards one's fellow men is essential – an understanding of the contradictions in man, and that he is a suffering creature but not one to be scorned.

This element of warm openness is technically tangible. It alone, if reciprocal, can enable the actor to undertake the most extreme efforts without any fear of being laughed at or humiliated. The type of work which creates such confidence makes words unnecessary during rehearsals. When at work, the beginnings of a sound or sometimes even a silence are enough to make oneself understood. What is born in the actor is engendered together, but in the end the result is far more a part of him than those results obtained at rehearsals in the "normal" theatre.

I think we are dealing here with an "art" of working which it is impossible to reduce to a formula and cannot simply be learnt. Just as any doctor does not necessarily make a good psychiatrist, not any producer can succeed in this form of theatre. The principle to apply as a piece of advice, and also a warning, is the following: "Primum non nocere" ("First, do not harm"). To express this in technical language: it is better to suggest by means of sound and gesture than to "act" in front of the actor or supply him with intellectual explanations; better to express oneself by means of a silence or a wink of the eye than by instructions, observing the stages in the psychological breakdown and collapse of the actor in order then to come to his aid. One must be strict, but like a father or older brother. The second principle is one common to all professions: if you make demands on your colleagues, you must make twice as many demands on yourself.

This implies that to work with the "holy" actor, there must be a producer who is twice as "holy": that is, a "super-saint" who, through his knowledge and intuition, breaks the bounds of the history of the theatre, and who is well acquainted with the latest results in sciences such as psychology, anthropology, myth interpretation and the history of religion.

All I have said about the wretchedness of the actor applies to the producer too. To develop the metaphor of the "courtesan actor", the equivalent among producers would be the "producer souteneur". And just as it is impossible to erase completely all traces of the "courtesan" in the "holy" actor, one can never completely eradicate the "souteneur" in the "holy" producer.

The producer's job demands a certain tactical **savoir faire,** namely in the art of leading. Generally speaking, this kind of power demoralizes. It entails the necessity of learning how to handle people. It demands a gift for diplomacy, a cold and inhuman talent for dealing with intrigues. These characteristics follow the producer like his shadow even in the poor theatre. What one might call the masochistic component in the actor is the negative variant of what is creative in the director in the form of a sadistic component. Here, as everywhere, the dark is inseparable from the light.

When I take sides against half-heartedness, mediocrity and the easy-come-easy-go attitude which takes everything for granted,

48

it is simply because we must create things which are firmly orientated towards either light or darkness. But we must remember that around that which is luminous within us, there exists a shroud of darkness which we can penetrate but not annihilate.

According to what you have been saying, "holiness" in the theatre can be achieved by means of a particular psychic discipline and various physical exercises. In the theatre schools and in traditional as well as experimental theatres, there is no such trend, no consistent attempt to work out or elaborate anything similar. How can we go about preparing the way for and training "holy" actors and producers? To what extent is it possible to create "monastic" theatres as opposed to the day-to-day "parochial" theatre?

I do not think that the crisis in the theatre can be separated from certain other crisis processes in contemporary culture. One of its essential elements – namely, the disappearance of the sacred and of its ritual function in the theatre – is a result of the obvious and probably inevitable decline of religion. What we are talking about is the possibility of creating a secular **sacrum** in the theatre. The question is, can the current pace in the development of civilization make a reality of this postulate on a collective scale?
I have no answer to this. One must contribute to its realization, for a secular consciousness in place of the religious one seems to be a psycho-social necessity for society. Such a transition ought to take place but that does not necessarily mean that it will. I believe that it is, in a way, an ethical rule, like saying that man must not act like a wolf towards his fellow men. But as we all know, these rules are not always applied.

In any case, I am sure that this renewal will not come from the dominating theatre. Yet, at the same time, there are and have been a few people in the official theatre who must be considered as secular saints: Stanislavski, for example. He maintained that the successive stages of awakening and renewal in the theatre had found their beginnings amongst amateurs and not in the circles of hardened, demoralized professionals. This was confirmed by Vakhtangov's experience; or to take an example from quite another culture, the Japanese No theatre which, owing to the technical ability it demands, might almost be described as a "super-profession", although its very structure makes it a semi-amateur theatre. From where can this renewal come? From people who are dissatisfied with conditions in the normal theatre, and who take it on themselves to create poor theatres with few actors, "chamber ensembles" which they might transform into institutes for the education of actors; or else from amateurs working on the boundaries of the professional theatre and who, on their own, achieve a technical standard which is far superior to that demanded by the prevailing theatre: in short, a few madmen who have nothing to lose and are not afraid of hard work.

It seems essential to me that an effort be made to organize secondary theatre schools. The actor begins to learn his profession too late, when he is already psychically formed and, worse still, morally moulded and immediately begins suffering from **arriviste** tendencies, characteristic of a great number of theatre school pupils.

Age is as important in the education of an actor as it is to a pianist or a dancer – that is, one should not be older than fourteen when beginning. If it were possible, I would suggest starting at an even earlier age with a four year technical course concentrating on practical exercises. At the same time, the pupil ought to receive an adequate humanistic education, aimed not at imparting an ample knowledge of literature, the history of the theatre and so on, but at awakening his sensibility and introducing him to the most stimulating phenomena in world culture.
The actor's secondary education should then be completed by four years' work as an apprentice actor with a laboratory en-

semble during which time he would not only acquire a good deal of acting experience, but would also continue his studies in the fields of literature, painting, philosophy, etc., to a degree necessary in his profession and not in order to be able to shine in snobbish society. On completion of the four years' practical work in a theatre laboratory, the student actor should be awarded some sort of diploma. Thus, after eight years' work of this kind, the actor should be comparatively well equipped for what lies ahead. He would not escape the dangers that threaten every actor, but his capacities would be greater and his character more firmly moulded. The ideal solution would be to establish institutes for research which again would be subject to poverty and rigourous authority. The cost of running such an institute would be a half of the amount swallowed up by a state aided provincial theatre. Its staff should be composed of a small group of experts specializing in problems associated with the theatre: e. g. a psychoanalyst and a social anthropologist. There should be a troupe of actors from a normal theatre laboratory and a group of pedagogs from a secondary theatre school, plus a small publishing house that would print the practical methodical results which would then be exchanged with other similar centres and sent to interested persons doing research in neighbouring fields. It is absolutely essential that all research of this kind be supervised by one or more theatre critics who, from the outside – rather like the Devil's Advocate – analyse the theatre's weaknesses and any alarming elements in the finished performances, basing their judgements on aesthetical principles identical to those of the theatre itself. As you know, Ludwik Flaszen has this task in our theatre.

How can such a theatre reflect our time? I am thinking of the content and analysis of present-day problems.

I shall answer according to our theatre's experience. Even though we often use classical texts, ours is a contemporary theatre in that it confronts our very roots with our current behaviour and stereotypes, and in this way shows us our "today" in perspective with "yesterday", and our "yesterday" with "today". Even if this theatre uses an elementary language of signs and sounds – comprehensible beyond the semantic value of the word, even to a person who does not understand the language in which the play is performed – such a theatre must be a national one since it is based on introspection and on the whole of our social super-ego which has been moulded in a particular national climate, thus becoming an integral part of it.

If we really wish to delve deeply into the logic of our mind and behaviour and reach their hidden layers, their secret motor, then the whole system of signs built into the performance must appeal to our experience, to the reality which has surprised and shaped us, to this language of gestures, mumblings, sounds and intonations picked up in the street, at work, in cafés – in short, all human behaviour which has made an impression on us.

We are talking about profanation. What, in fact, is this but a kind of tactlessness based on the brutal confrontation between our declarations and our daily actions, between the experience of our forefathers which lives within us and our search for a comfortable way of life or our conception of a struggle for survival, between our individual complexes and those of society as a whole?

This implies that every classical performance is like looking at oneself in a mirror, at our ideas and traditions, and not merely the description of what men of past ages thought and felt.

Every performance built on a contemporary theme is an encounter between the superficial traits of the present day and its deep roots and hidden motives. The performance is national because it is a sincere and absolute search into our historical ego; it is realistic because it is an excess of truth; it is social because it is a challenge to the social being, the spectator.

Theatre is an Encounter

In June 1967, during Expo 67 in Canada, Jerzy Grotowski attended an international theatre symposium held in Montreal. During his stay he had the following interview with Naim Kattan which was published in **Arts et Lettres, Le Devoir** (July 1967). Translation: Robert Dewsnap.

In one of your texts, you have said that the theatre can exist without costumes or scenery, without music or lighting effects – and even without a text. You added: "In the development of the theatrical art, the text was one of the last elements to be added." There is, in your view, only one element with which the theatre cannot dispense, and that is the actor. Since the Commedia dell'Arte, however, there have been playwrights. Can the producer of today disregard the theatrical traditions of several centuries? What place do you, as a producer, give to the text?

It is not the core of the problem. The core is the encounter. The text is an artistic reality existing in the objective sense. Now, if the text is sufficiently old and if it has preserved all its force for today – in other words, if this text contains certain concentrations of human experiences, representations, illusions, myths and truths which are still actual for us today – then, the text becomes a message which we receive from previous generations. In the same sense, the new text can be a sort of prism which reflects our experiences. The entire value of the text is already present once it has been written; this is literature, and we may read plays as part of "literature". In France, plays published in book form are given the title of **Theatre** – a mistake in my opinion, because this is not theatre but dramatic literature. Faced with this literature, we can take up one of two positions: either, we can illustrate the text through the interpretation of the actors, the **mise en scène,** the scenery, the play situation ... In that case, the result is not theatre, and the only living element in such a performance is the literature. Or, we can virtually ignore the text, treating it solely as a pretext, making interpolations and changes, reducing it to nothing. I feel that both of these two solutions are false ones, because in both cases we are not fulfilling our duties as artists, but trying to comply with certain rules – and art doesn't like rules. Masterpieces are always based on the transcendence of rules. Though of course, the test is in the performance.

Take for example Stanislavski. His plan was to realise all the intentions of the dramatists, to create a literary theatre. And when we speak of the style of Chekhov, we are really alluding to the style of Stanislavski's productions of plays by Chekhov. As a matter of fact, Chekhov himself protested about this when he said: "I have written vaudevilles and Stanislavski has put sentimental dramas on the stage." Stanislavski was a genuine artist and he realised, involuntarily, **his** Chekhov and not an objective Chekhov. Meyerhold in his turn proposed, in all possible good faith, an autonomous theatre vis-à-vis literature. But I think his is the only example in the history of the theatre of a performance so deeply rooted in the spirit of Gogol, in his deepest meaning. Meyerhold's **The Inspector General** was a sort of collage of the texts of Gogol. Consequently, it is not our fine ideas but our practice which constitutes the test.

What is the task of the theatre in respect to literature?

The core of the theatre is an encounter. The man who makes an act of self-revelation is, so to speak, one who establishes contact

56

with himself. That is to say, an extreme confrontation, sincere, disciplined, precise and total – not merely a confrontation with his thoughts, but one involving his whole being from his instincts and his unconscious right up to his most lucid state.

The theatre is also an encounter between creative people. It is I myself, as producer, who am confronted with the actor, and the self-revelation of the actor gives me a revelation of myself. The actors and myself are confronted with the text. Now, we cannot express what is objective in the text, and in fact it is only those texts which are really weak that give us a unique possibility of interpretation. All the great texts represent a sort of deep gulf for us. Take Hamlet: books without number have been devoted to this character. Professors will tell us, each for himself, that they have discovered an objective Hamlet. They suggest to us revolutionary Hamlets, rebel and impotent Hamlets, Hamlet the outsider, etc. But there is no objective Hamlet. The work is too great for that. The strength of great works really consists in their catalystic effect: they open doors for us, set in motion the machinery of our self-awareness. My encounter with the text resembles my encounter with the actor and his with me. For both producer and actor, the author's text is a sort of scalpel enabling us to open ourselves, to transcend ourselves, to find what is hidden within us and to make the act of encountering the others; in other words, to transcend our solitude. In the theatre, if you like, the text has the same function as the myth had for the poet of ancient times. The author of **Prometheus** found in the Prometheus myth both an act of defiance and a spring-board, perhaps even the source of his own creation. But his **Prometheus** was the product of his personal experience. That is all one can say about it; the rest is of no importance. I repeat, one can play the text in its entirety, one can change its whole structure or make a sort of collage. One can, on the other hand, make adaptations and interpolations. In neither case is it a question of theatrical creation but of literature. Brecht has given examples of treatments of other authors, and so did Shakespeare. As for me, I wish to make neither a literary interpretation nor a literary treatment, for both are beyond my competence, my field being that of theatrical creation. For me, a creator of theatre, the important thing is not the words but what we do with these words, what gives life to the inanimate words of the text, what transforms them into "the Word". I will go further: the theatre is an act engendered by human reactions and impulses, by contacts between people. This is both a biological and a spiritual act. Let us be quite clear that I don't mean making love to the audience – that would involve making oneself into a sort of article of sale.

All the same, to put plays on stage you still have to choose texts and authors. What is your method of procedure? How do you choose one play rather than another, or one playwright rather than another?

The encounter proceeds from a fascination. It implies a struggle, and also something so similar in depth that there is an identity between those taking part in the encounter. Every producer must seek encounters which suit his own nature. For me this means the great romantic poets of Poland. But it also means Marlowe and Calderon. I should make quite clear that I am very fond of texts which belong to a great tradition. For me, these are like the voices of my ancestors and those voices which come to us from the sources of our European culture. These works fascinate me because they give us the possibility of a sincere confrontation – a brutal and brusque confrontation between on the one hand the beliefs and experiences of life, of previous generations and, on the other, our own experiences and our own prejudices.

Is there, in your opinion, a relationship between a dramatic work and the age in which it took shape?

Yes, there is indeed a relationship between the historical context of the text, between the age and the text itself. But it is not the context which decides our inclination and our will to confront ourselves with these works. It is the context of my experiences today which decides my choice. Let us take an example – Homer. Why do we study the **Iliad** and the **Odyssey** nowadays? Is it to acquaint ourselves with the cultural and social life of the people of that age? Perhaps, yes – but that's a job for the professors. In the perspective of art, the works are always alive. The characters of the **Odyssey** are still actual because there are still pilgrims. We too are pilgrims. Their pilgrimage is different from ours, and it is for this reason that it throws a new light on our own condition.

One should not make too many speculations in the field of art. Art is not the source of science. It is the experience which we take upon ourselves when we open ourselves to others, when we confront ourselves with them in order to understand ourselves – not in the scientific sense of re-creating the context of an epoch in history, but in an elementary and human sense. And in the long procession of suffering mothers it is not the historical context of Niobe which interests us. Of course, the past is present inasmuch as we can still hear and understand its voice. Niobe's voice may seem to us a little strange. It is doubtless rather different from that of the mother weeping over her children at Auschwitz, and this difference constitutes the whole historical context. It is hidden; and if we try to separate it, to underline it and accentuate it, then we lose everything since artistic experience is an open and direct one.

Akropolis: Treatment of the Text

This text by Ludwik Flaszen, literary adviser to the Theatre Laboratory, has been published in: Pamietnik Teatralny (Warsaw, 3. 1964), Alla Ricerca del Teatro Perduto (Marsilio Editori, Padova, 1965) and Tulane Drama Review (New Orleans, T 27, 1965). Translation: Simone Sanzenbach.

Akropolis was produced by Jerzy Grotowski. His main collaborator in this production was the well known polish stage designer, Josef Szajna, who also designed the costumes and props. The scenic architecture was by Jerzy Gurawski.

Principal characters: Jacob, the harpist, leader of the dying tribe - Zygmunt Molik; Rebecca Cassandra - Rena Mirecka; Isaac - Antoni Jaholkowski; Angel Paris - Zbigniew Cynkutis or Mieczyslaw Janowski; Esau - Ryszard Cieslak.

Wyspianski's drama has been modified in parts to adjust to the purpose of the director. The few interpolations and changes in the original text do not, however, detract from the style of the poet. The balance of the text has been somewhat altered by the deliberately obsessive repetition of certain phrases such as "our Akropolis" or "the cemetery of the tribes". This liberty is justified because these phrases are the motifs around which the play revolves. The prologue is an excerpt from one of Wyspianski's letters, referring to the "Akropolis" as the symbol of the highest point of any specific civilization.

Of all the plays Grotowski has directed, **Akropolis** is the least faithful to its literary original. The poetic style is the only thing which belongs to the author. The play was transposed for stage conditions totally different from those planned by the poet. In a sort of counterpoint pattern, it has been enriched with associations of ideas which bring out, as a secondary result of the enterprise, a specific concept of the technique: the verbal flesh of the work had to be transplanted and grafted on the viscera of foreign stage setting. The transplant had to be done with such skill that the words would seem to grow spontaneously from the circumstances imposed by the theatre.

The action of the play takes place in Cracow cathedral. On the night of the Resurrection, the statues and the characters in the tapestries relive scenes from the Old Testament and antiquity, the very roots of European tradition.

The author conceived his work as a panoramic view of the Mediterranean culture whose main currents are represented in this Polish Akropolis. In this idea of the "cemetery of the tribes", to quote Wyspianski, the concept of the director and that of the poet coincide. They both want to represent the sum total of a civilization and test its values on the touchstone of contemporary experience. To Grotowski, contemporary means the second half of the twentieth century. Hence his experience is infinitely more cruel than Wyspianski's and the century-old values of European culture are put to a severe test. Their merging point is no longer the peaceful resting place of the old cathedral where the poet dreamed and meditated in solitude on the history of the world. They clash in the din of an extreme world in the midst of the polyglot confusion where our century has projected them: in an extermination camp. The characters re-enact the great moments of our cultural history; but they bring to life not the figures immortalized in the monuments of the past, but the fumes and emanations from Auschwitz.

It is indeed a "cemetery of the tribes", but not the same as the one where the old Galician poet wandered and dreamed. It is literally a "cemetery", complete, perfect, paradoxical; one which transforms the most daring poetic figures into realities. "Our Akropolis", blind with hope, will not see the Resurrection of Christ-Apollo: he has been left behind, in the mysterious outer reaches of collective experience. The drama formulates a question: what happens to human nature when it faces total violence? The struggle of Jacob with the Angel and the back-breaking labor of the inmates, Paris' and Helen's love duet and the derisive screams of the prisoners, the Resurrection of Christ and the ovens – a civilization of contrast and corruption ...

Trapped at its roots, this image of the human race gives rise to horror and pity. The tragi-comedy of rotten values has been substituted for the luminous apotheosis which concluded the philosophic-historic drama of the old poet. The director has shown that suffering is both horrible and ugly. Humanity has been reduced to elemental animal reflexes. In a maudlin intimacy, murderer and victim appear as twins.

All the luminous points are deliberately snuffed out in the stage presentation. The ultimate vision of hope is squashed with blasphemous irony. The play as it is presented can be interpreted as a call to the ethical memory of the spectator, to his moral unconscious. What would become of him if he were submitted to the supreme test? Would he turn into an empty human shell? Would he become the victim of those collective myths created for mutual consolation?

The performance: from fact to metaphor

The play is conceived as a poetic paraphrase of an extermination camp. Literal interpretation and metaphor are mixed as in a daydream. The rule of the Theatre Laboratory is to distribute the action all over the theatre and among the spectators. These, however, are not expected to take part in the action. For **Akropolis,** it was decided that there would be no direct contact between actors and spectators: the actors represent those who have been initiated in the ultimate experience, they are the dead; the spectators represent those who are outside of the circle of initiates, they remain in the stream of everyday life, they are the living. This separation, combined with the proximity of the spectators, contributes to the impression that the dead are born from a dream of the living. The inmates belong in a nightmare and seem to move in on the sleeping spectators from all sides. They appear in different places, simultaneously or consecutively, creating a feeling of vertigo and threatening ubiquity.

In the middle of the room stands a huge box. Metallic junk is heaped on top of it: stovepipes of various lengths and widths, a wheelbarrow, a bathtub, nails, hammers. Everything is old, rusty, and looks as if it had been picked up from a junkyard. The reality of the props is rust and metal. From them, as the action progresses, the actors will build an absurd civilization; a civilization of gas chambers, advertised by stovepipes which will decorate the whole room as the actors hang them from strings or nail them to the floor. Thus one passes from fact to metaphor.

Costumes

The costumes are bags full of holes covering naked bodies. The holes are lined with material which suggests torn flesh; through the holes one looks directly into a torn body. Heavy wooden shoes for the feet; for the heads, anonymous berets. This is a poetic version of the camp uniform. Through their similarity the costumes rob men of their personality, erase the distinctive signs which indicate sex, age, and social class. The actors become completely identical beings. They are nothing but tortured bodies.

The inmates are the protagonists and, in the name of a higher, unwritten law, they are their own torturers. The merciless conditions of the extermination camp constitute the milieu of their lives. Their work crushes them with its size and its futility; rhythmical signals are given by the guards; the inmates call out in screams. But the struggle for the right to vegetate and to love goes on at its everyday pace. At each command the human wrecks, barely alive, stand up erect like well-disciplined soldiers. The throbbing rhythm of the play underscores the building of the new civilization; the work expresses the inmate's stubborn will to live, which is constantly reaffirmed in every one of their actions.

There is no hero, no character set apart from the others by his own individuality. There is only the community, which is the image

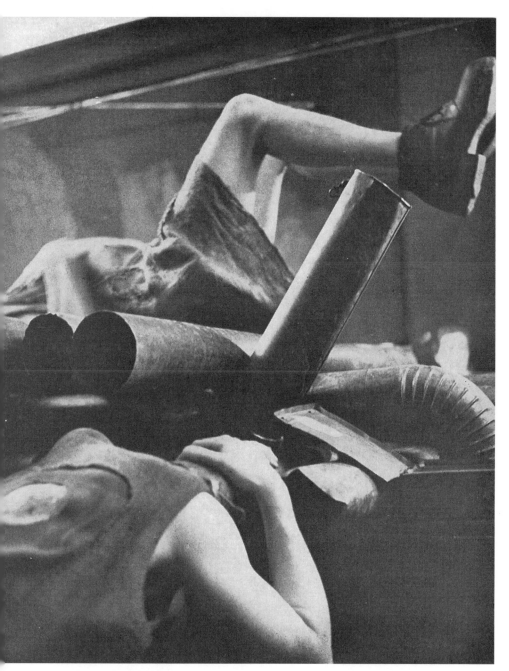

1. **Akropolis:** Dialogue between two monuments **(Rena Mirecka and Zbigniew Cynkutis).**
   Photo: Teatr-Laboratorium.

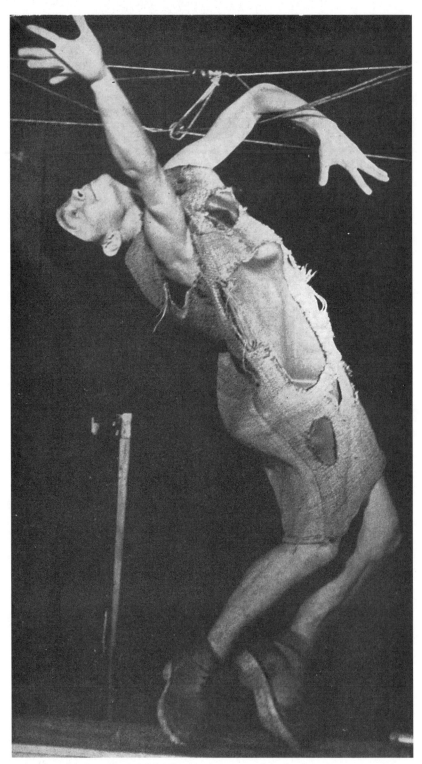

2. **Akropolis:** Esau **(Ryszard Cieslak)** sings the praises of the freedom of a hunter's life.
Photo: **Teatr-Laboratorium.**

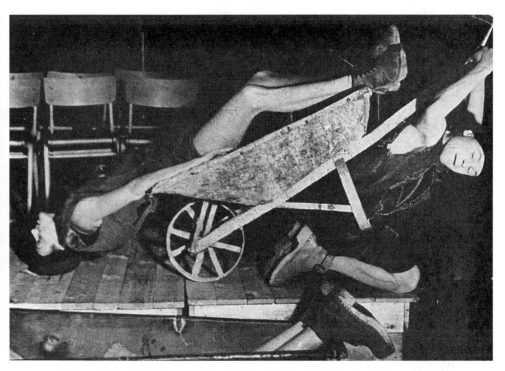

3. **Akropolis:** The fight between Jacob and the Angel **(Zbigniew Cynkutis and Zygmunt Molik).** **Photo: Teatr-Laboratorium.**

4. **Akropolis:** The prisoners rest. **Photo: Teatr-Laboratorium.**

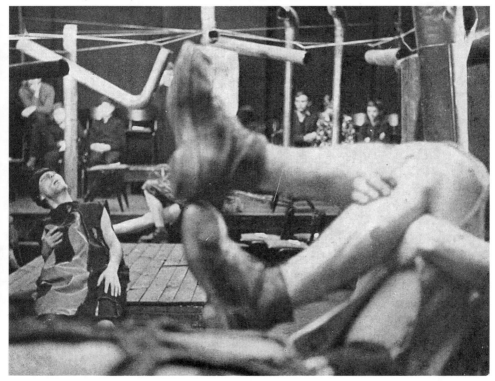

5. **Akropolis:** The march to work to build the Akropolis of our time: an extermination camp
(**Zbigniew Cynkutis and Ryszard Cieslak**). Photo: Teatr-Laboratorium.

6. **Akropolis:** The wedding procession of Rebecca and Jacob. Jacob **(Zygmunt Molik)** leads the way, tenderly carrying a piece of pipe as a substitute for his bride. **Photo: Teatr-Laboratorium.**

7. **Akropolis:** Jacob, the harpist, leader of the dying tribe **(Zygmunt Molik).**
   Photo: Teatr-Laboratorium.

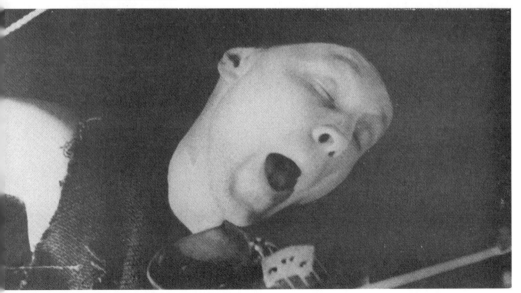

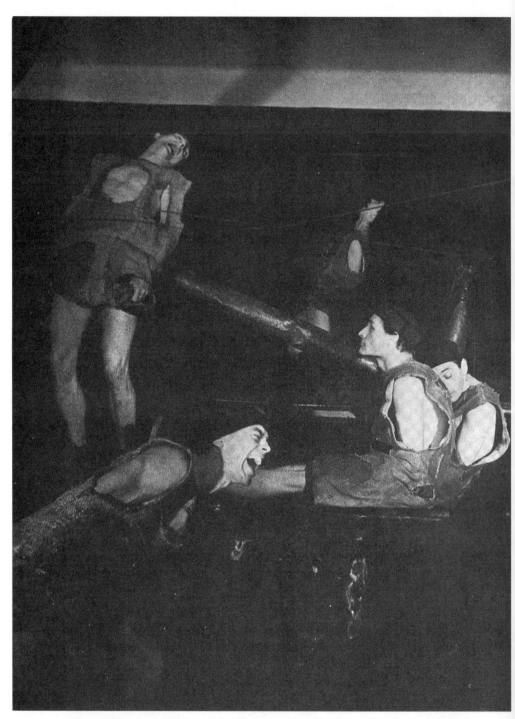

8. **Akropolis:** Paris and Helen display the bliss of sensual love, but here Helen is a man. Their lyrical cooing is interrupted by the unanimous sneers of the other prisoners.
Photo: Teatr-Laboratorium.

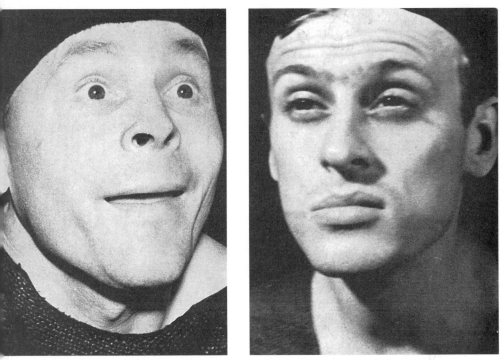

9. **Akropolis:** Masks created solely by the facial muscles **(Zygmunt Molik, Zbigniew Cynkutis, Rena Mirecka). Photo: Teatr-Laboratorium.** 10.

11. 12.

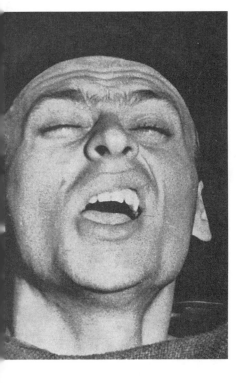

13. **Akropolis:** The Saviour has come. A headless corpse is believed to be Christ and the prisoners, ecstatic in their joy, follow him to salvation. **Photo: Teatr-Laboratorium.**

14. **Akropolis:** The descent to salvation: the crematory. **Photo: Teatr-Laboratorium.**

of the whole species in an extreme situation. In the fortissimos, the rhythm is broken into a climax of words, chants, screams, and noises. The whole thing seems multishaped and misshapen; it dissolves, then re-forms itself into a shivering unity. It is reminiscent of a drop of water under a microscope.

Myth and reality

During the pauses in the work, the fantastic community indulges in daydreams. The wretches take the names of biblical and Homeric heroes. They identify with them and act, within their limitations, their own versions of the legends. It is transmutation through the dream, a phenomenon known to communities of prisoners who, when acting, live a reality different from their own. They give a degree of reality to their dreams of dignity, nobility, and happiness. It is a cruel and bitter game which derides the prisoners' own aspirations as they are betrayed by reality.

Jacob tramples his future father-in-law to death while asking for Rachel's hand in marriage. Indeed, his relationship to Laban is not governed by patriarchal law but by the absolute demands of the right to survive. The struggle between Jacob and the Angel is a fight between two prisoners: one is kneeling and supports on his back a wheelbarrow in which the other lies, head down and dropping backward. The kneeling Jacob tries to shake off his burden, the Angel, who bangs his own head on the floor. In his turn the Angel tries to crush Jacob by hitting his head with his feet. But his feet hit, instead, the edge of the wheelbarrow. And Jacob struggles with all his might to control his burden. The protagonists cannot escape from each other. Each is nailed to his tool; their torture is more intense because they cannot give vent to their mounting anger. The famous scene from the Old Testament is interpreted as that of two victims torturing each other under the pressure of necessity, the anonymous power mentioned in their argument.

73

Paris and Helen express the charm of sensuous love; but Helen is a man. Their love duet is conducted to the accompaniment of the snickering laughter of the assembled prisoners. A degraded eroticism rules the world where privacy is impossible. Their sexual sensitivity has become that of any monosexual community, the army for example. Similarly Jacob directs his expression of tenderness toward compensatory objects: his bride is a stove pipe wrapped into a piece of rag for a veil. Thus equipped, he leads the nuptial procession solemnly followed by all the prisoners singing a folksong. At the high point of this improvised ceremony, the clear sound of an altar bell is heard, suggesting naïvely and somewhat ironically a dream of simple happiness.

The despair of men condemned without hope of reprieve is revealed: four prisoners press their bodies against the walls of the theatre like martyrs. They recite the prayer of hope in the help of God pronounced by the Angel in Jacob's dream. One detects in the recitation the ritual grief and the traditional lament of the Bible. They suggest the Jews in front of the Wall of Lamentation. There is, too, the aggressive despair of the condemned who rebel against their fate: Cassandra. One of the prisoners, a female, walks out of the ranks at roll call. Her body wriggles hysterically; her voice is vulgar, sensuous, and raucous; she expresses the torments of a self-centered soul. Shifting suddenly to a tone of soft complaint, she announces with obvious relish what fate holds in store for the community. Her monologue is interrupted by the harsh and guttural voices of the prisoners in the ranks who count themselves. The clipped sounds of the roll call replace the cawing of crows called for in Wyspianski's text.

As for hope, the group of human wrecks, led by the Singer, finds its Savior. The Savior is a headless, bluish, badly mauled corpse, horribly reminiscent of the miserable skeletons of the concentration camps. The Singer lifts the corpse in a lyrical gesture, like a priest lifting the chalice. The crowd stares religiously and follows the leader in a procession. They begin to sing a Christmas hymn to honor the Savior. The singing becomes louder, turns into an ecstatic lament torn by screams and hysterical laughter. The procession circles around the huge box in the center of the room; hands stretch toward the Savior, eyes gaze adoringly. Some stumble, fall, stagger back to their feet and press forward around the Singer. The procession evokes the religious crowds of the Middle Ages, the flagellants, the haunting beggars. Theirs is the ecstasy of a religious dance. Intermittently, the procession stops and the crowd is quiet. Suddenly the silence is shattered by the devout litanies of the Singer, and the crowd answers. In a supreme ecstasy, the procession reaches the end of its peregrination. The Singer lets out a pious yell, opens a hole in the box, and crawls into it dragging after him the corpse of the Savior. The inmates follow him one by one, singing fanatically. They seem to throw themselves out of the world. When the last of the condemned men has disappeared, the lid of the box slams shut. The silence is very sudden; then after a while a calm, matter-of-fact voice is heard. It says simply, "They are gone, and the smoke rises in spirals." The joyful delirium has found its fulfillment in the crematorium. The end.

Props as dynamic orchestration

The strictest independence from props is one of the main principles of the Theatre Laboratory. It is absolutely forbidden to introduce in the play anything which is not already there at the very beginning. A certain number of people and objects are gathered in the theatre. They must be sufficient to handle any of the play's situations.

There are no "sets" in the usual sense of the word. They have been reduced to the objects which are indispensable to the dramatic action. Each object must contribute not to the meaning but to the dynamics of the play; its value resides in its various uses. The stovepipes and the metallic junk are used as settings

75

and as a concrete, three-dimensional metaphor which contributes to the creation of the vision. But the metaphor originates in the function of the stovepipes; it stems from the activity which it later supersedes as the action progresses. When the actors leave the theatre, they leave behind the pipes which have supplied a concrete motivation for the play.

Each object has multiple uses. The bathtub is a very pedestrian bathtub; on the other hand it is a symbolical bathtub: it represents all the bathtubs in which human bodies were processed for the making of soap and leather. Turned upside down, the same bathtub becomes the altar in front of which an inmate chants a prayer. Set up in a high place, it becomes Jacob's nuptial bed. The wheelbarrows are tools for daily work; they become strange hearses for the transportation of the corpses; propped against the wall they are Priam's and Hecuba's thrones. One of the stovepipes, transformed by Jacob's imagination, becomes his grotesque bride.

This world of objects represents the musical instruments of the play: the monotonous cacophony of death and senseless suffering – metal grating against metal, clanging of the hammers, creaking of the stovepipes through which echoes a human voice. A few nails rattled by an inmate evoke the altar bell. There is only one real musical instrument, a violin. Its leitmotiv is used as a lyrical and melancholy background to a brutal scene, or as a rhythmical echo of the guards' whistles and commands. The visual image is almost always accompanied by an acoustic one. The number of props is extremely limited; each one has multiple functions. Worlds are created with very ordinary objects, as in children's play and improvised games. We are dealing with a theatre caught in its embryonic stage, in the middle of the creative process when the awakened instinct chooses spontaneously the tools of its magic transformation. A living man, the actor, is the creative force behind it all.

76

The poor theatre

In the poor theatre the actor must himself compose an organic mask by means of his facial muscles and thus each character wears the same grimace throughout the whole play. While the entire body moves in accordance with the circumstances, the mask remains set in an expression of despair, suffering and indifference. The actor multiplies himself into a sort of hybrid being acting out his role polyphonically. The different parts of his body give free rein to different reflexes which are often contradictory, while the tongue denies not only the voice, but also the gestures and the mimicry.

All the actors use gestures, positions, and rhythms borrowed from pantomime. Each has his own silhouette irrevocably fixed. The result is a depersonalization of the characters. When the individual traits are removed, the actors become stereotypes of the species.

The means of verbal expression have been considerably enlarged because all means of vocal expression are used, starting from the confused babbling of the very small child and including the most sophisticated oratorical recitation. Inarticulate groans, animal roars, tender folksongs, liturgical chants, dialects, declamation of poetry: everything is there. The sounds are interwoven in a complex score which brings back fleetingly the memory of all the forms of language. They are mixed in this new Tower of Babel, in the clash of foreign people and foreign languages meeting just before their extermination.

The mixture of incompatible elements, combined with the warping of language, brings out elementary reflexes. Remnants of sophistication are juxtaposed to animal behavior. Means of expression literally "biological" are linked to very conventional compositions. In **Akropolis** humanity is forced through a very fine sieve: its texture comes out much refined.

77

Dr Faustus: Textual Montage

Not one word of Marlowe's original text was changed, but the script was rearranged into a "montage" where the succession of scenes was modified, new scenes were created and some of the original ones were omitted. These are notes on this production as Eugenio Barba recorded them. This text has been published in **Tulane Drama Review** (New Orleans, T 24, 1964) and **Alla Ricerca del Teatro Perduto** (Marsilio Editori, Padova, 1965). Translation: Richard Schechner.

Dr Faustus was produced by **Jerzy Grotowski**. The costumes were designed by **Waldemar Krygier** and the scenic architecture by **Jerzy Gurawski**.

Principal characters: Faustus – **Zbigniew Cynkutis;** the androgynous Mephistopheles – **Rena Mirecka** and **Antoni Jaholkowski;** Benvolio – **Ryszard Cieslak.**

Faustus has one hour to live before his martyrdom of hell and eternal damnation. He invites his friends to a last supper, a public confession where he offers them episodes from his life as Christ offered his body and blood. Faustus welcomes his guests – the audience – as they arrive and asks them to sit at two long tables on the sides of the room. Faustus takes his place at a third, smaller table like the prior in a refectory. The feeling is that of a medieval monastery, and the story apparently concerns only monks and their guests. This is the underlying archetype of the text. Faustus and the other characters are dressed in the habits of different orders. Faustus is in white; Mephistopheles is in black, played simultaneously by a man and a woman; other characters are dressed as Franciscans. There are also two actors seated at the tables with the audience, dressed in everyday clothes. More about them later.

This is a play based on a religious theme. God and the Devil intrigue with the protagonists – that is why the play is set in a monastery. There is a dialectic between mockery and apotheosis. Faustus is a saint and his saintliness shows itself as an absolute desire for pure truth. If the saint is to become one with his sainthood, he must rebel against God, Creator of the world, because the laws of the world are traps contradicting morality and truth.

Stipendium peccati mors est. Ha! Stipendium, etc.
The reward of sin is death. That's hard.
Si peccasse negamus, fallimur
Et nulla est in nobis veritas.
If we say we have no sin,
We deceive ourselves, and there's no truth in us.
Why then belike we must sin,
And so consequently die.
Ay, we must die an everlasting death.

(I,i,39–47)

Whatever we do – good or bad – we are damned. The saint is not able to accept as his model this God who ambushes man. God's laws are lies, He spies on the dishonor in our souls the better to damn us. Therefore, if one wants sainthood, one must be against God.

But what must the saint care for? His soul, of course. To use a modern expression, his own self-consciousness. Faustus, then, is not interested in philosophy or theology. He must reject this kind of knowledge and look for something else. His research begins precisely in his rebellion against God. But how does he rebel? By signing his pact with the Devil. In fact, Faustus is not only a saint but a martyr – even more so than the Christian saints and martyrs, because Faustus expects no reward. On the contrary, he knows that his due will be eternal damnation.

Here we have the archetype of the saint. The role is played by an actor who looks young and innocent – his psycho-physical characteristics resemble St. Sebastian's. But this St. Sebastian is anti-religious, fighting God.

The dialectic of mockery and apotheosis consists then of a conflict between lay sainthood and religious sainthood, deriding our usual ideas of a saint. But at the same time this struggle appeals to our contemporary "spiritual" commitment, and in this we have the apotheosis. In the production, Faustus' actions are a grotesque paraphrase of a saint's acts; and yet, he reveals at the same time the poignant pathos of a martyr.

The text is rearranged in such a way that Act V, scene two of Marlowe's script – where Faustus argues with the three scholars – opens the production. Faustus, full of humility, his eyes empty, lost in the imminence of his martyrdom, greets his guests while seated at his small table, his arms open as on the Cross. Then he begins his confession. What we usually call virtues, he calls sin – his theological and scientific studies; and what we call sin, he calls virtue – his pact with the Devil. During this confession, Faustus' face glows with an inner light.

When Faustus begins to talk about the Devil and his first magic tricks, he enters into the second reality (flashbacks). The action then shifts to the two tables where Faustus evokes the episodes of his life, a kind of biographical travelogue.

Scene 1. Faustus greets his guests.

Scene 2. Wagner announces that his master is soon to die.

Scene 3. A monologue in which Faustus publicly confesses as sins his studies and exalts as a virtue his pact with the Devil.

Scene 4. In a flashback, Faustus begins to tell the story of his life. First there is a monologue recalling the moment when he decided to renounce theology and take up magic. This interior struggle is represented by a conflict between an owl, who symbolizes the erudite personality, and a donkey, whose stubborn inertia is opposed to the owl's learning.

Scene 5. Faustus talks to Cornelius and Valdes, who come to initiate him in magic. Cornelius turns a table into a confessional booth. As he confesses Faustus, granting him absolution, Faustus begins his new life. The spoken text often contradicts its interpretation; for example, these lines describe the pleasures of magic. Then Cornelius reveals the magic ceremonies to Faustus and teaches him an occult formula – which is nothing other than a well-known Polish religious hymn.

Scene 6. Faustus in the forest. By imitating a gust of wind, the tumbling of leaves, the noises of the night, the cries of nocturnal animals, Faustus finds himself singing the same religious hymn invoking Mephistopheles.

Scene 7. The appearance of Mephistopheles (the Annunciation). Faustus is on his knees in a humble pose. Mephistopheles, on one leg, a soaring angel, sings his lines accompanied by an angelic choir. Faustus tells him that he is ready to give his soul to the Devil in exchange for twenty-four years of life against God.

Scene 8. The mortification of Faustus. A masochistic scene provoked by the arguments of the Good and Bad Angels. Faustus rubs his own spit in his face, knocks his head against his knees, rips at his genitals – all while reciting his lines in a calm voice.

Scene 9. During a walk Faustus tells Mephistopheles of his decision to give him his soul.

Scene 10. Faustus' baptism. Before signing the contract, Faustus is almost drowned in a river (the space between the tables). Thus he is purified and ready for his new life. Then the female Mephistopheles promises to grant all his wishes. She comforts Faustus by rocking him in her lap (the Pietà).

Scene 11. Signing the pact. Faustus reads his contract with Mephistopheles in a commercial tone. But his gestures reveal a struggle to suppress the anguish which torments him. Finally, overcoming his hesitation, he tears his clothes off in a kind of self-rape.

Scene 12. The double Mephistopheles, using liturgical gestures, shows Faustus his new vestments.

Scene 13. Scene with his "devil-wife." Faustus treats her as if she were a book which held all the secrets of nature.

> Now would I have a book where I might see all
> Characters and planets of the heavens, that I might know
> Their motions and dispositions.
> ....
> ... Wherein I might see all plants, herbs, and trees that
> Grow upon the earth.
>
> (1604 Quarto,I,v,618–620, 634–635)

The saint examines the slut as if he were carefully reading a book. He touches all the parts of her body and reads them as "planets," "plants," etc.

Scene 14. Mephistopheles tempts Faustus. In Scene 13 the young saint has begun to suspect that the Devil is also in God's service. Scene 14 corresponds to a real break in reality, Mephistopheles, at this point in the production, is like a police informer. He takes three roles: Mephistopheles himself, the Good Angel, and the Bad Angel. It is not by accident that the double Mephistopheles is dressed as a Jesuit who tempts Faustus to act sinfully. But when Faustus begins to understand the consequences, he calmly evaluates the Good Angel's words. In this scene, Mephistopheles, as the Good Angel, offers Faustus a meeting with God. They act as if it were late at night in a monastery, and two dissatisfied monks were talking quietly out of everyone's hearing. But Faustus refuses to repent anything.

Scene 15. Astrological discussions. Mephistopheles plays the role of a loyal servant exalting the harmony and perfection of his master's creation in duplicating the sound of the celestial spheres. The conversation is interrupted by two guests who talk of beer and whores. These are the two actors who have been sitting for the whole performance among the spectators. They have played all the farce roles (Robin, Vintner, Dick, Carter, Scholars, Old Man, etc.). In their scenes they represent the banality that marks our everyday life. One of these comic scenes (with the Horse-

Courser) is acted right after Faustus asks Mephistopheles, "Now tell me who made the world?" Our daily platitudes are themselves arguments against God. Our saint demands to know who is responsible for the creation of such a world. Mephistopheles, servant of God's evil urge, falls into a real panic and refuses to answer: "I will not."

Scene 16. One by one Lucifer shows the Seven Deadly Sins to Faustus. Faustus absolves them as Christ absolved Mary Magdalene. The Seven Deadly Sins are played by the same persons: the double Mephistopheles.

Scene 17. Faustus is transported to the Vatican by two dragons, the double Mephistopheles.

Scene 18. Faustus, invisible at the feet of the Pope, is present at a banquet in St. Peter's. The banquet table is made of the bodies of the double Mephistopheles, who recites the Ten Commandments. Faustus slaps the Pope, breaking him of his pride and vanity. He transforms the Pope into a humble man – this is Faustus' miracle.

Scene 19. At the palace of Emperor Charles V, Faustus performs miracles in the tradition of the popular legends. He splits the earth and brings forth Alexander the Great. Then Faustus outwits Benvolio, a courtier who wants to kill him: Benvolio's rage is directed against the tables – he actually dismantles the table-tops, and turns sections of the tables over, all the while thinking he is dismembering Faustus. Then Faustus turns Benvolio into a little child.

Scene 20. Return to the present – Faustus' last supper. Faustus picks up his conversation with his guests. Upon the urging of a friend he conjures up Helen of Troy, unmasking by comic allusions the female biological functions. Helen begins to make love to him – immediately she gives birth to a baby. Then, while in this erotic position, she becomes the wailing infant. Finally she is transformed into a greedy baby at suck.

Scene 21. The double Mephistopheles shows Paradise to Faustus. This would have been his had he followed God's precepts: a good, calm, and pious death. Then they show him the hell that awaits him: a convulsive and violent death.

Scene 22. The final scene. Faustus has but a few minutes to live. A long monologue which represents his last, and most outrageous, provocation of God.

> Ah Faustus,
> Now hast thou but one bare hour to live,
> And then thou must be damned perpetually!
> (V,ii,130–131)

In the original text, this monologue expresses Faustus' regret for having sold his soul to the Devil; he offers to return to God. In the production, this is an open struggle, the great encounter between the saint and God. Faustus, using gestures to argue with Heaven, and invoking the audience as his witness, makes suggestions that would save his soul, if God willed it, if He were truly merciful and all-powerful enough to rescue a soul at the instant of its damnation. First Faustus proposes that God stop the celestial spheres – time – but in vain.

> Stand still, you ever-moving spheres of heaven,
> That time may cease and midnight never come.
> (V,ii,133–134)

He addresses God, but answers himself, "O, I'll leap up to my God! Who pulls me down?" (V, ii, 142). Faustus observes an interesting phenomenon: the sky is covered with the blood of Christ, and just one half drop would save him. He demands salvation:

> See, see, where Christ's blood streams in the firmament!
> One drop would save my soul, half a drop! ...
> (V,ii,143–144)

But Christ vanishes, even as Faustus implores him, and this prompts Faustus to say to his guests, "Where is it now? 'Tis gone." (V, ii, 147). Then God's angry face appears, and Faustus is frightened:

> ... And see where God
> Stretcheth out his arm and bends his ireful brows!
> (V,ii,147–148)

Faustus wants the earth to open and swallow him, and he throws himself to the ground.

> Mountains and hills, come, come, and fall on me,
> And hide me from the heavy wrath of God.
> (V,ii,149–150)

But the earth is deaf to his prayers and he rises crying, "O no, it will not harbor me!" (V, ii, 153). The sky then resonates with the Word and in all the corners of the room the hidden actors, reciting like monks, chant prayers like the Ave Maria and the Pater Noster. Midnight sounds. Faustus' ecstasy is transformed into his Passion. The moment has come when the saint – after having shown his guests the guilty indifference, yes, even the sin of God – is ready for his martyrdom: eternal damnation. He is in a rapture, his body is shaken by spasms. The ecstatic failure of his voice becomes at the moment of his Passion a series of inarticulate cries – the piercing, pitiable shrieks of an animal caught in a trap. His body shudders, and then all is silence. The double Mephistopheles, dressed as two priests, enters and takes Faustus to hell.

Mephistopheles lugs Faustus away on his back, holding him by the feet, the saint's head down near the ground, his hands trailing on the floor. Thus he goes to his eternal damnation, as a sacrificial animal is carried, as one is dragged to the Cross.

The female Mephistopheles follows humming a sad march which becomes a melancholy religious song (the Mother of Sorrows following her Son to Calvary). From the saint's mouth come raucous cries; these inarticulate sounds are not human. Faustus is no longer a man, but a panting animal, an unclaimed, once-human wreck moaning without dignity. The saint against God has attained his "summit," he has lived God's cruelty. He is the victor – morally. But he has paid the full price of that victory: eternal martyrdom in hell where all is taken from him, even his dignity.

15. **Dr Faustus:** General view of the scenic arrangement. Faustus **(Zbigniew Cynkutis)** awaits the arrival of his guests (the spectators). **Photo: Opiola-Moskwiak.**

16. **Dr Faustus:** The double androgynous Mephistopheles **(Rena Mirecka and Antoni Jahol-kowski). Photo: Opiola-Moskwiak.**

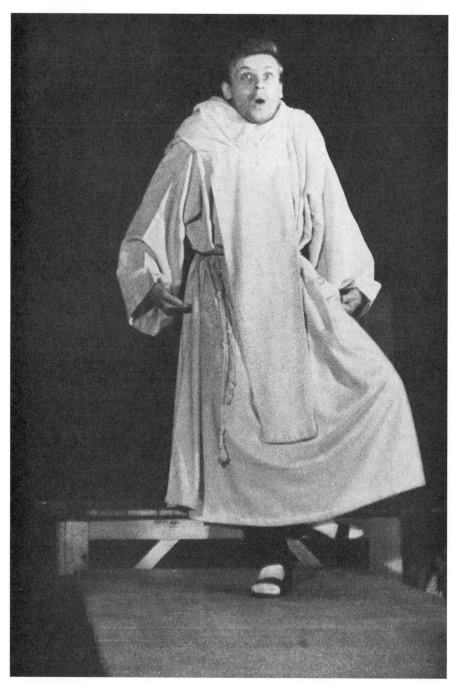

17. **Dr Faustus:** Monologue by Faustus in which he decides to take up magic **(Zbigniew Cynkutis).**
Photo: **Opiola-Moskwiak.**

18. **Dr Faustus:** Faustus is initiated into magic **(Zbigniew Cynkutis and Ryszard Cieslak).**
Photo: **Opiola-Moskwiak.**

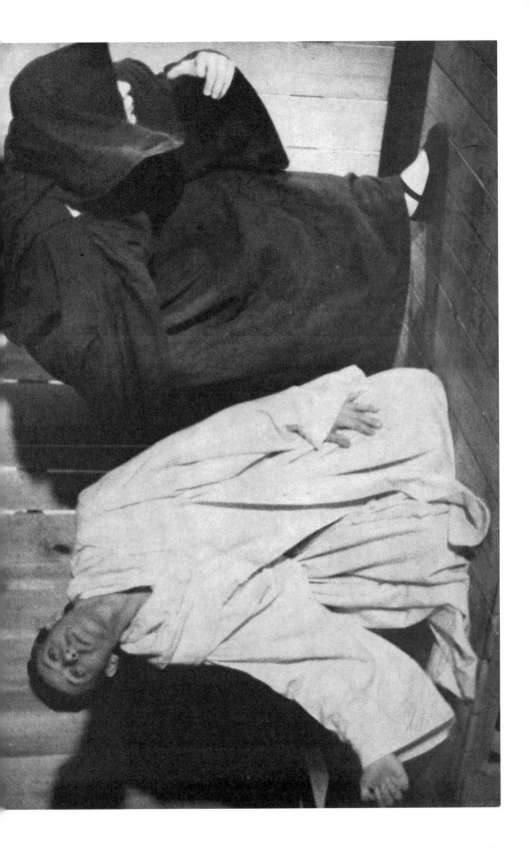

19. **Dr Faustus:** One of the Seven Deadly Sins **(Rena Mirecka). Photo: Opiola-Moskwiak.**

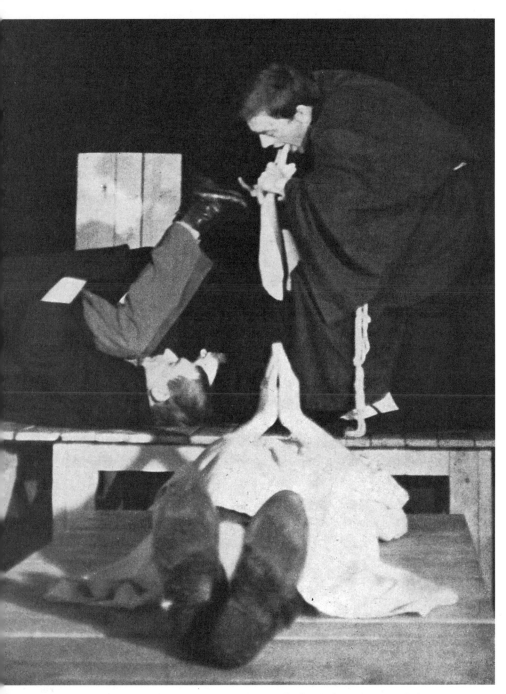

20. **Dr Faustus:** Faustus, invisible, attends the Pope's meal. The Pope's throne is composed of the double Mephistopheles **(Antoni Jaholkowski, Rena Mirecka, Zbigniew Cynkutis and Ryszard Cieslak). Photo: Opiola-Moskwiak.**

21. **Dr Faustus:** Benvolio **(Ryszard Cieslak),** in a fury, destroys the set, attempting to kill Faustus. **Photo: Opiola-Moskwiak.**

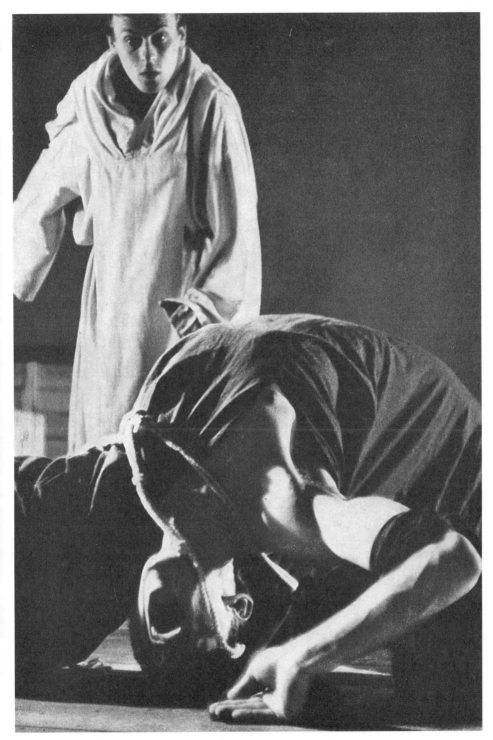

22. **Dr Faustus:** Faustus appeases Benvolio **(Zbigniew Cynkutis and Ryszard Cieslak). Photo: Opiola-Moskwiak.**

23. **Dr Faustus:** The double Mephistopheles carries Faustus to hell **(Antoni Jaholkowski, ⎯⎯→ Zbigniew Cynkutis and Rena Mirecka). Photo: Opiola-Moskwiak.**

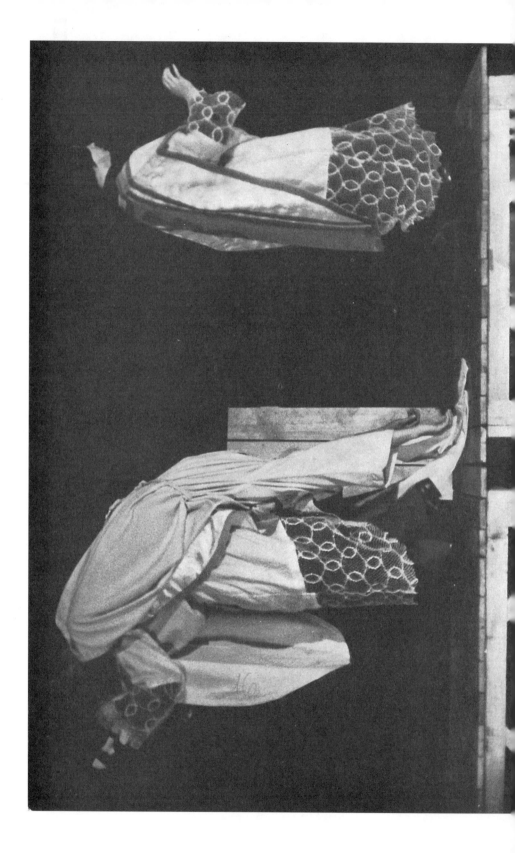

The Constant Prince

This introduction by **Ludwik Flaszen** appeared in the polish programme.

The Constant Prince was produced by **Jerzy Grotowski**. The costumes were designed by **Walde-mar Krygier** and the scenic architecture by **Jerzy Gurawski**.

Principal characters: the Constant Prince – **Ryszard Cieslak**; the King – **Antoni Jaholkowski;** Fenixana – **Rena Mirecka;** Tarudant, the persecutor – **Maja Komorowska;** Muley, the persecutor – **Mieczyslaw Janowski;** the first prisoner – **Stanislaw Scierski.**

The scenario of this performance is based on the text by the great seventeenth century Spanish playwright, Calderon de la Barca, in its excellent Polish transcription by Julius Slowacki, the eminent Romantic poet. The producer, however, does not mean to play **The Constant Prince** as it is. He aims at giving his own vision of the play, and the relation of his scenario to the original text is that of a musical variation to the original musical theme.

In the opening scene, the First Prisoner collaborates with his persecutors. Lying on a ritual bed, he is first symbolically castrated and then, after being dressed in a uniform, becomes "one of the company". The performance is a study of the phenomenon of "inflexibility" which does not consist in the manifestation of force, dignity and courage. To the people around him who look upon him rather as on a strange animal, the Second Prisoner – the Prince – opposes only passivity and kindness, referring to a higher spiritual order. He seems to offer no opposition to the ugly and villainous doings of the people around him and does not even discuss with them. They are simply beyond his consideration. He refuses to be one of them. Thus the Prince's enemies who would appear to hold him in their power, in fact have no influence over him. While submitting to their evil doings, he preserves his independence and purity to the point of ecstasy.

97

The arrangement of stage and audience resembles something between an arena and an operating-theatre. One may think of what one sees below in terms of some cruel sport in an ancient Roman arena or a surgical operation as portrayed in Rembrandt's "Anatomy of Dr. Tulp".

The people surrounding the Prince – an alienated and peculiar society – wear togas, breeches and top-boots to show that they take pleasure in making use of their power, that they are confident of their judgement, particularly when concerning people of a different kind. The Prince wears a white shirt – an ingenuous symbol of purity – and a red coat which can at times be changed into a shroud. At the end of the play he is naked, with nothing to defend himself but his own human identity.

The feelings of society towards the Prince are not uniformly hostile. They are rather an expression of a sense of difference and strangeness combined with a sort of fascination, and this combination contains in it the possibility of such extreme reflexes as violence and adoration. Everyone wants to have the martyr for himself and at the end of the performance they fight for him as if he were a precious object. Meanwhile the hero is constantly faced with endless contradictions and submitted to the will of his enemies. Once the deed is done, the people who tormented the Prince to death regret their action and bewail his lot. The birds of prey turn into turtle-doves.

Finally he becomes a living hymn in homage to human existence, in spite of his having been persecuted and stupidly humiliated. The Prince's ecstasy is his suffering which he can endure only by offering himself to the truth as if in an act of love. Thus the performance, paradoxically enough, is an attempt to get over the tragic pose. It consists in casting off all the elements which might force us to accept the tragic aspect.

The producer believes that although he is not faithful to Calderon's text to the letter, he nevertheless retains the inner meaning of the play. The performance is a transposition of the profound antinomies and most characteristic traits of the baroque era such as its visionary aspect, its music, its appreciation of the concrete and its spiritualism.

The performance is also a kind of exercise that makes possible the verification of Grotowski's method of acting. All is moulded in the actor: in his body, in his voice and in his soul.

24. **The Constant Prince:** General view of the scenic arrangement. The spectators-peepers look on as at
a forbidden act. In the centre, the first prisoner **(Stanislaw Scierski). Photo: Bernand.**

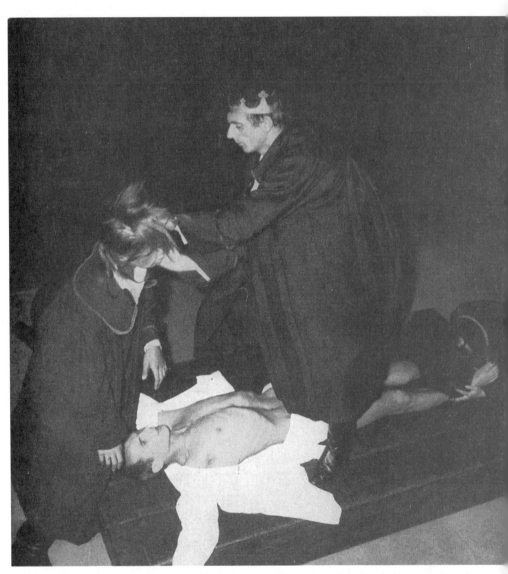

25. **The Constant Prince:** Treatment of the first prisoner. Fascination and rivalry grip his persecutors who assimilate him into their clan. **Photo: Bernand.**

26. **The Constant Prince:** Pietà. The Constant Prince is embraced by one of his persecutors. ⟶
Photo: Teatr-Laboratorium.

27. **The Constant Prince:** The persecutors confess their sins to their victim **(Rena Mirecka and Ryszard Cieslak). Photo: Teatr-Laboratorium.**

28. **The Constant Prince:** The Constant Prince **(Ryszard Cieslak),** refusing to collaborate with his persecutors, is tortured while the courtiers pray. **Photo: Teatr-Laboratorium.**

29.

30.

29 -30. **The Constant Prince:** A ball is held at th court. The cries of the tortured form th music of the minuet **(Rena Mirecka and Ry zard Cieslak). Photo: Bernand.**

31. **The Constant Prince:** Before martyrising the Constant Prince, the king lends him his crown in order to obtain his absolution. **Photo: Teatr-Laboratorium.**

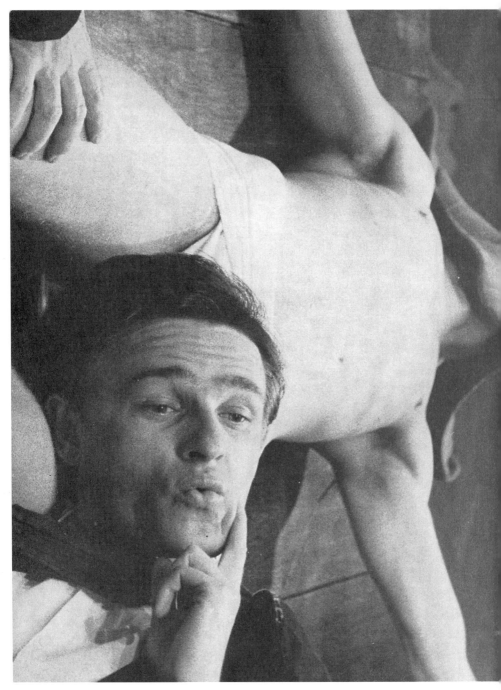

32. **The Constant Prince:** The Constant Prince is dead. Now is the time to apotheosize him and kill others in his name. **Photo: Samosiuk.**

Monologues of Ryszard Cieslak as the Constant Prince: steps towards his summit

Photo: Teatr-Laboratorium. 33–40. ⟶

In my opinion the force and, moreover, the success of **The Constant Prince** are mainly due to the principal character. In the actor's creation, the essential elements of Grotowski's theory take precise tangible forms which can be verified not merely in the demonstration of his method, but also in the beautiful fruits it produces.

The essence of this does not in reality reside in the fact that the actor makes amazing use of his voice, nor in the way that he uses his almost naked body to sculpt mobile forms that are striking in their expressiveness; nor is it in the way that the technique of the body and voice form a unity during the long and exhausting monologues which vocally and physically border on acrobacy. It is a question of something quite different.

We have always followed – and often acknowledged – the remarkable technical results achieved by Grotowski in his work with the actor. We have nevertheless retained a certain scepticism with regard to the arguments he uses which compare the work of the actor to a psychic act of transgression, an exploration, a sublimation, a displacement of deep-lying psychic substances. However, when faced with the creation of Ryszard Cieslak, this scepticism is called in question.

In my profession as a theatre critic I have never yet felt the desire to use that dreadfully banal and overworked expression which, in this particular case, is quite simply true: this creation is "inspired". I cannot help considering this word with a certain amount of surprise, examining it through a magnifying glass, but if it still has a legitimate place in the world of theatrical criticism, I certainly could not find a better opportunity to use it. Until now, I accepted with reserve the terms such as "secular holiness", "act of humility", "purification" which Grotowski uses. Today I admit that they can be applied perfectly to the character of the Constant Prince. A sort of psychic illumination emanates from the actor. I cannot find any other definition. In the culminating moments of the role, everything that is technique is as though illuminated from within, light, literally imponderable. At any moment the actor will levitate ... He is in a state of grace. And all around him this "cruel theatre" with its blasphemies and excesses is transformed into a theatre in a state of grace.

JOSEF KELERA
ODRA XI, 1965.

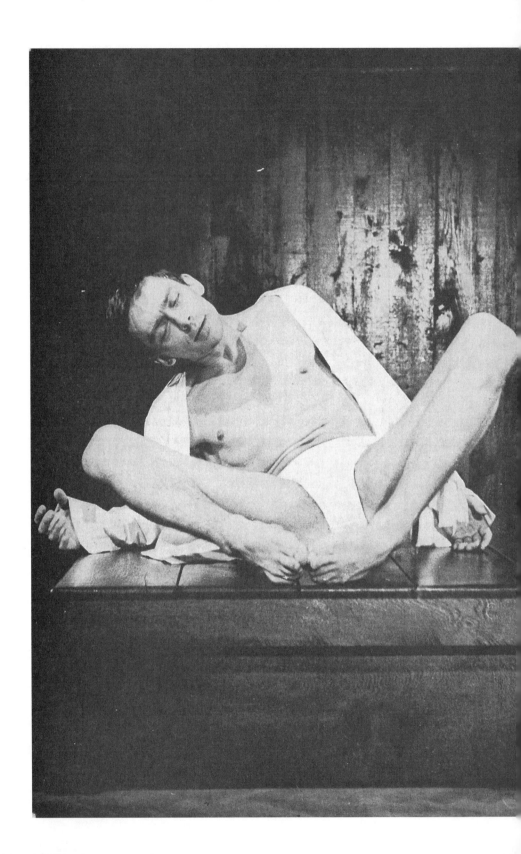

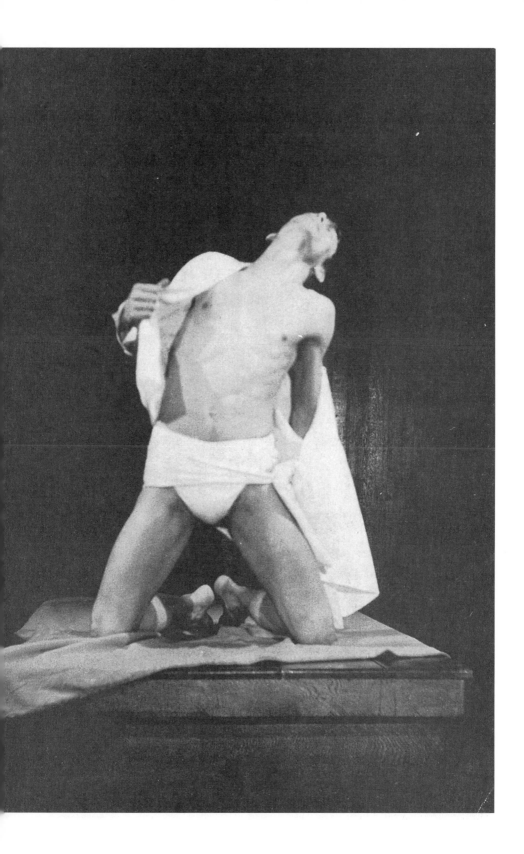

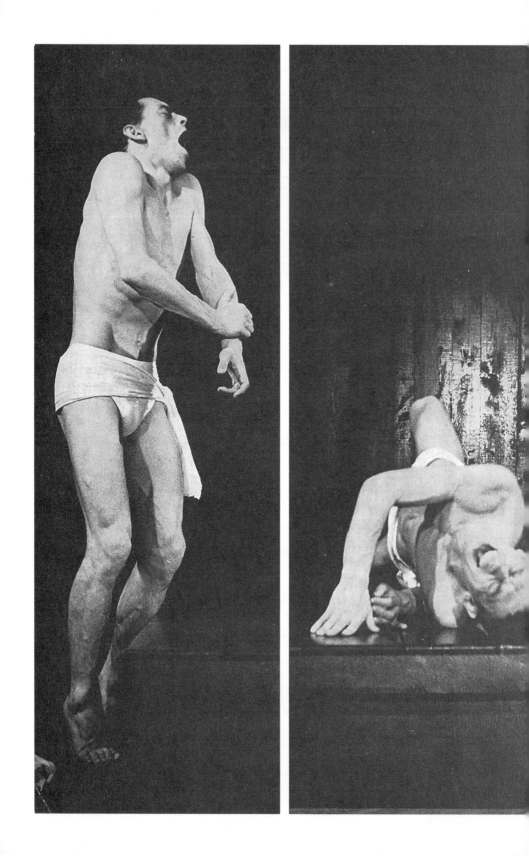

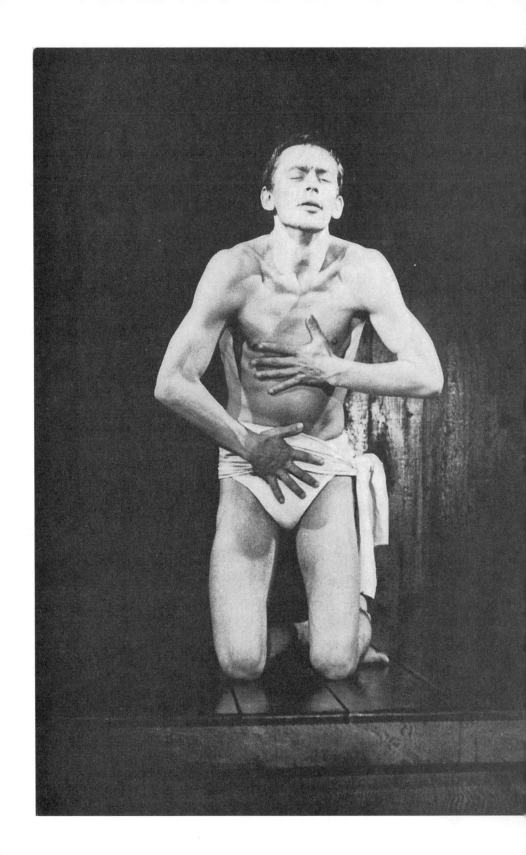

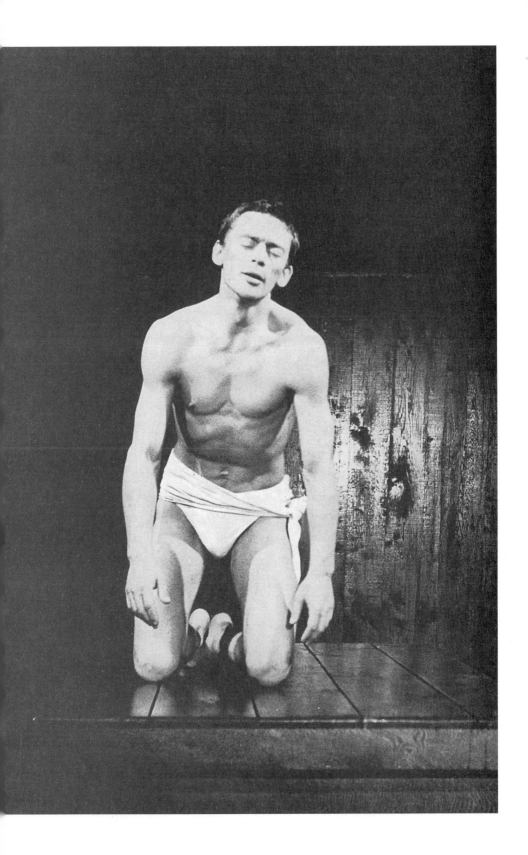

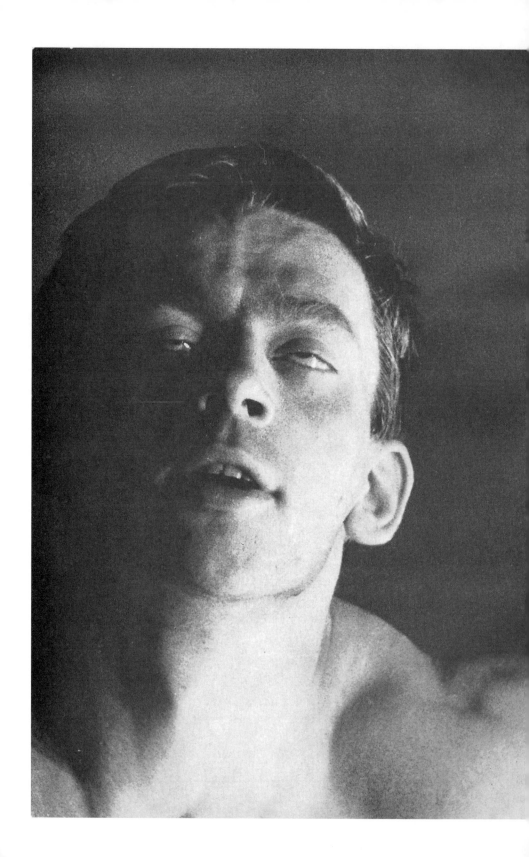

He Wasn't Entirely Himself

This article by Jerzy Grotowski has been published in **Les Temps Modernes** (Paris, April 1967) and **Flourish,** the newspaper of the Royal Shakespeare Theatre Club (Summer 1967).

Stanislavski was compromised by his disciples. He was the first great creator of a method of acting in the theatre, and all those of us who are involved with theatre problems can do no more than give personal answers to the questions he raised. When, in numerous European theatres, we watch performances inspired by the "Brecht theory," and are obliged to fight against utter boredom because the lack of conviction of both actors and producers takes the place of the so-called "Verfremdungseffekt", we think back to Brecht's own productions. They were perhaps less true to his theory but, on the other hand, very personal and subversive as they were, they showed a deep professional knowledge and never left us in a state of lassitude.

We are entering the age of Artaud. The "theatre of cruelty" has been canonised, i.e. made trivial, swapped for trinkets, tortured in various ways. When an eminent creator with an achieved style and personality, like Peter Brook, turns to Artaud, it's not to hide his own weaknesses, or to ape the man. It just happens that at a given point of his development he finds himself in agreement with Artaud, feels the need of a confrontation, **tests** Artaud, and retains whatever stands up to this test. He remains himself. But as for the wretched performances one can see in the theatrical

117

avant-garde of many countries, these chaotic, aborted works, full of a so-called cruelty which would not scare a child, when we see all these happenings which only reveal a lack of professional skill, a sense of groping, and a love of easy solutions, performances which are only violent on the surface (they should hurt us but do not manage to) – when we see these sub-products whose authors call Artaud their spiritual father, then we think that perhaps there is cruelty indeed, but only towards Artaud himself.

The paradox of Artaud lies in the fact that it is impossible to carry out his proposals. Does this mean that he was wrong? Certainly not. But Artaud left no concrete technique behind him, indicated no method. He left visions, metaphors. This was surely an expression of Artaud's personality and is partly the result of lack of time and means to put the things he glimpsed into practice. It also comes from what we might call Artaud's mistake, or at least his peculiarity: as he probed subtly, in an a-logical, almost invisible and intangible way, Artaud used a language which was almost as intangible and fleeting. Yet micro-organisms are studied with a precision instrument, the microscope. Whatever is imperceptible demands precision.

Artaud spoke of the magic of the theatre, and the way he conjured it up leaves images which touch us in some way. Perhaps we don't understand them completely, but we realise he was after a theatre transcending discursive reason and psychology. And when, one fine day, we discover that the essence of the theatre is found neither in the narration of an event, nor in the discussion of a hypothesis with an audience, nor in the representation of life as it appears from outside, nor even in a vision – but that the theatre is an act carried out **here and now** in the actors' organisms, in front of other men, when we discover that theatrical reality is instantaneous, not an illustration of life but something linked to life **only by analogy**, when we realise all this, then we ask ourselves the question: wasn't Artaud talking about just this and nothing else?

For when in the theatre we dispose of the tricks of make-up and costume, stuffed bellies and false noses, and when we propose to the actor that he should transform himself before the spectator's eyes using only his inner impulses, his body, when we state that the magic of the theatre consists in this transformation **as it comes to birth,** we once more raise the question: did Artaud ever suggest any other kind of magic?

Artaud speaks of the "cosmic trance". This brings back an echo of the time when the heavens were emptied of their traditional inhabitants and themselves became the object of a cult. The "cosmic trance" inevitably leads to the "magic theatre". Yet Artaud explains the unknown by the unknown, the magic by the magic. I do not know what is meant by the "cosmic trance" for, generally speaking, I do not believe that the cosmos can, in a physical sense, become a transcendental point of reference for man. The points of reference are others. Man is one of them.

Artaud opposed the discursive principle in theatre, i. e. the entire French theatre tradition. But we can't accept him as a pioneer In this. Many central European and Eastern theatres have a living tradition of non-discursive theatre. And how do we rate Vakhtangov or Stanislavski?

Artaud refused a theatre which was content to illustrate dramatic texts; he claimed the theatre should be a creative art in itself, and not just duplicate what literature was doing. This was a sign of great courage and consciousness on his part, for he wrote in a language in which the complete works of playwrights were not entitled "Plays" or "Comedies" but "The Theatre of Molière", or "The Theatre of Montherlant". Yet the idea of an autonomous theatre came to us much earlier, from Meyerhold in Russia.

119

Artaud intended to suppress the barrier between actors and audience. This seems striking, but note that he neither proposed to abolish the stage separate from the auditorium, nor to seek a different structure adapted to each new production thus creating a real basis for confrontation between the two "ensembles" formed by the actors and the spectators. He simply proposed to put the audience in the centre and play in all four corners of the room. This is no elimination of the stage/audience barrier, but the replacement of the classical dolls' theatre by another rigid structure. And years before all these ideas of Artaud, decisive steps in this direction had already been taken by Reinhard, Meyerhold in his production of the Mystery plays, and again later by Syrkus in Poland with his already elaborated conception of a "simultaneous theatre".

Thus we have withdrawn Artaud's supposed merits in order to restore them to their true fathers. It might be thought we are preparing a scene of martyrdom, stripping Artaud of his rags just as he stripped Beatrice Cenci in his production. But there is a difference between stripping someone to torture them, and doing so to find out who they really are. The fact that others have made similar suggestions in other places cannot alter the vital fact that Artaud made his discoveries himself, through his own suffering, the prism of his personal obsessions, and that as far as his own country goes, he virtually invented everything.

Must it be repeated yet again that if Artaud had had at his disposal the necessary material, his visions might have developed from the undefined to the defined and he might even have converted them into a form or, better still, a technique? He would then have been in a position to anticipate all the other reformers, for he had the courage and the power to go beyond the current discursive logic. All this could have happened, but never did.

Artaud's secret, above all, is to have made particularly fruitful mistakes and misunderstandings. His description of Balinese theatre, however suggestive it may be for the imagination, is really one big mis-reading. Artaud deciphered as "cosmic signs" and "gestures evoking superior powers" elements of the performance which were concrete expressions, specific theatrical letters in an alphabet of signs universally understood by the Balinese.

The Balinese performance for Artaud was like a crystal ball for a fortune-teller. It brought forth a totally different performance which slumbered in his depths, and this work of Artaud's provoked by the Balinese theatre gives us an image of his great creative possibilities. As soon as he moves from description to theory however, he starts explaining magic by magic, cosmic trance by cosmic trance. It is a theory which can mean whatever you require.

But in his description he touches something essential, of which he is not quite aware. It is the true lesson of the sacred theatre; whether we speak of the medieval European drama, the Balinese, or the Indian Kathakali: this knowledge that spontaneity and discipline, far from weakening each other, mutually reinforce themselves; that what is elementary feeds what is constructed and vice versa, to become the real source of a kind of acting that glows. This lesson was neither understood by Stanislavski, who let natural impulses dominate, nor by Brecht, who gave too much emphasis to the construction of a role.

Artaud intuitively saw myth as the dynamic centre of the theatre performance. Only Nietzsche was ahead of him in this domain. He also knew that transgression of the myth renewed its essential values and "became an element of menace which re-established the derided norms" (L. Flaszen). He did not however take account of the fact that, in our age, when all languages intermingle, the community of the theatre cannot possibly **identify** itself with myth, because there is no single faith. Only a **confrontation** is possible.

121

Artaud dreamed of producing new myths through the theatre, but this beautiful dream was born from his lack of precision. For although the myth forms the basis or framework for the experience of entire generations, it is for the subsequent generations to create it and not the theatre. At the most, the theatre could have contributed to the crystallization of the myth. But then it would have been too similar to current ideas to be creative.

A confrontation is a "trying out", a testing of whatever is a traditional value. A performance which, like an electrical transformer, adjusts our experience to those of past generations (and vice versa), a performance conceived as a combat against traditional and contemporary values (whence "transgression") – this seems to me the only real chance for myth to work in the theatre. An honest renewal can only be found in this double game of values, this attachment and rejection, this revolt and submissiveness.

Nevertheless, Artaud was a prophet. His texts conceal such a special and complex web of forecasts, such impossible allusions, visions which are so suggestive and metaphors which seem, in the long run, to possess a certain soundness. For all this is bound to happen. No one knows how, but it is inevitable. And it does happen.

We shout with triumph when we discover silly misunderstandings in Artaud. The sign which, in oriental theatre, is simply a part of a universally known alphabet, cannot – as Artaud would have it – be transferred to European theatre in which every sign has to be born separately in relation to familiar psychological or cultural associations, before becoming something quite different. All his divisions of breathing into masculine, feminine and neuter are just misinterpretations of oriental texts, and in practice, so imperceptiple they cannot be distinguished. His study of the "athletics of feelings" has certain shrewd insights, but in practical work would lead to stereotyped gestures, one for each emotion.

122

Yet he does touch on something which we may be able to reach by a different route. I mean the very crux of the actor's art: that what the actor achieves should be (let's not be afraid of the name) a total act, that he does whatever he does with his entire being, and not just one mechanical (and therefore rigid) gesture of arm or leg, not any grimace, helped by a logical inflection and a thought. No thought can guide the entire organism of an actor in any living way. It must stimulate him, and that is all it really can do. Without committment, his organism stops living, his impulses grow superficial. Between a total reaction and a reaction guided by a thought there is the same difference as between a tree and a plant. In the final result we are speaking of the impossibility of separating spiritual and physical. The actor should not use his organism to illustrate a "movement of the soul", he should accomplish this movement with his organism.

Artaud teaches us a great lesson which none of us can refuse. This lesson is his sickness. Artaud's misfortune is that his sickness, paranoia, differed from the sickness of the times. Civilisation is sick with schizophrenia, which is a rupture between intelligence and feeling, body and soul. Society couldn't allow Artaud to be ill in a different way. They looked after him, tortured him with electro-shock treatment, trying to make him acknowledge discursive and cerebral reason: i. e. to take society's sickness into himself. Artaud defined his illness remarkably in a letter to Jacques Rivière: "I am not entirely myself". He was not merely himself, he was someone else. He grasped half of his own dilemma: how to be oneself. He left the other half untouched: how to be whole, how to be complete.

He couldn't bridge the deep gulf between the zone of visions (intuitions) and his conscious mind, for he had given up everything orderly, and made no attempt to achieve precision or mastery of things. Instead he made his chaos and his self-division objective. His chaos was an authentic image of the world. It wasn't a therapy but a diagnosis, at least in the eyes of other people.

His chaotic outbursts were holy, for they enabled others to reach self-knowledge.

Among his successors, the chaos is in no sense holy, nor sufficiently determined: it has no reason for existing save to conceal something unfinished, to hide an infirmity. Artaud gave this chaos expression, which is quite another matter.

Artaud puts forward the idea of a great release, a great transgression of conventions, a purification by violence and cruelty; he affirms that the evocation of blind powers on stage ought to protect us from them in life itself. But how can we ask them to protect us in this way when it's obvious they do nothing of the kind? It's not in the theatre that dark powers can be controlled; more likely that these powers will turn the theatre to their own ends. (Although I don't think they are concerned about the theatre, since they have massive means of domination already at their disposal.) The theatre in the end neither protects us nor leaves us unprotected. I don't believe that the explosive portrayal of Sodom and Gomorrah on a stage calms or sublimates in any way the sinful impulses for which those two towns were punished.

And yet when Artaud speaks of release and cruelty we feel he's touching a truth we can verify in another way. We feel that an actor reaches the essence of his vocation whenever he commits an act of sincerity, when he unveils himself, opens and gives himself in an extreme, solemn gesture, and does not hold back before any obstacle set by custom and behaviour. And further, when this act of extreme sincerity is modelled in a living organism, in impulses, a way of breathing, a rhythm of thought and the circulation of blood, when it is ordered and brought to consciousness, not dissolving into chaos and formal anarchy – in a word, when this act accomplished through the theatre is **total,** then even if it doesn't protect us from the dark powers, at least it enables us to respond totally, that is, begin to exist. For each day we only react with half our potential.

If I speak of "a total act", it's because I have the feeling that there is an alternative to "the theatre of cruelty". But Artaud stands as a challenge to us at this point: perhaps less because of his work than his idea of salvation through the theatre. This man gave us, in his martyrdom, a shining proof of the theatre as therapy. I have found two expressions in Artaud which deserve attention. The first is a reminder that anarchy and chaos (which he needed as a spur for his own character) should be linked to a sense of order, which he conceived in the mind, and not as a physical technique. Still, it's worth quoting this phrase for the sake of Artaud's so-called disciples: "Cruelty is rigour".

The other phrase holds the very foundation of the actor's art of extreme and ultimate action. "Actors should be like martyrs burnt alive, still signalling to us from their stakes". Let me add that these signals must be articulated, and they cannot just be gibberish or delirious, calling out to everything and nothing – unless a given work demands precisely that. With such a proviso, we affirm that this quotation contains in an oracular style, the whole problem of spontaneity and discipline, this **conjunction of opposites** which gives birth to the total act.

Artaud was a great theatre-poet, which means a poet of the possibilities of theatre and not of dramatic literature. Like the mythical prophet Isaiah, he predicts for the theatre something definitive, a new meaning, a new possible incarnation. "Then Emmanuel was born". Like Isaiah, Artaud knew of Emmanuel's coming, and what it promised. He saw the image of it through a glass, darkly.

Methodical Exploration

This article by Jerzy Grotowski was written to explain the aim of his Institute. It has been published in **Tygodnik Kulturalny** (Warsaw, 17/1967). Translation: Amanda Pasquier and Judy Barba.

I

What is the Bohr Institute?

Bohr and his team founded an institution of a quite extraordinary nature. It is a meeting place where physicists from different countries experiment and take their first steps into the "no man's land" of their profession. Here they compare their theories and draw from the "collective memory" of the Institute.

This "memory" keeps a detailed inventory of all the research done, including even the most audacious, and is continually enriched with new hypotheses and results obtained by the physicists.

The late Niels Bohr and his collaborators tried to discover in this ocean of common research certain guiding trends. They provided an instigation and inspiration in the sphere of their discipline. Thanks to the work of the men to whom they gave both a welcome and a stimulation, they were able to compile essential data and profit from the industrial potentialities of the most developed countries throughout the world.

The Bohr Institute has fascinated me for a long time as a model illustrating a certain type of activity. Of course the theatre is not a scientific discipline, and even less so the art of the actor on whom my attention is centred. However, the theatre, and in particular the technique of the actor, cannot – as Stanislavski

127

maintained – be based solely on inspiration or on other such unpredictable factors as talent explosion, the sudden and surprising growth of creative possibilities, etc. Why? Because unlike the other artistic disciplines, the actor's creation is imperative: i.e. situated within a determined lapse of time and even at a precise moment. An actor cannot wait for a surge of talent nor for a moment of inspiration.

How, then, can these factors be made to appear when they are needed? By obliging the actor who wishes to be creative to master a method.

II

In our opinion, the conditions essential to the art of acting are the following, and should be made the object of a methodical investigation:

a) To stimulate a process of self-revelation, going back as far as the subconscious, yet canalizing this stimulus in order to obtain the required reaction.
b) To be able to articulate this process, discipline it and convert it into signs. In concrete terms, this means to construct a score whose notes are tiny elements of contact, reactions to the stimuli of the outside world: what we call "give and take".
c) To eliminate from the creative process the resistances and obstacles caused by one's own organism, both physical and physical (the two forming a whole).

How can the laws which govern such personal and individual processes be expounded objectively? How can one merely define objective laws without giving a "recipe" (for all "recipes" only end in banality)?
We believe that in order to fulfil this individuality, it is not a matter of learning new things, but rather of ridding oneself of old habits.

For each individual actor it must be clearly established what it is that blocks his intimate associations, thus causing his lack of decision, the chaos of his expression and his lack of discipline; what prevents him from experiencing the feeling of his own freedom, that his organism is completely free and powerful, and that nothing is beyond his capabilities. In other words, how can the obstacles be eliminated?

We take away from the actor that which shuts him off, but we do not teach him how to create – for example how to play Hamlet, in what consists the tragic gesture, how to act a farce – for it is precisely in this "how" that the seeds of banality and of the clichés that defy creation are planted.
To do research such as this is to place oneself already on the borders of scientific disciplines such as phonology, psychology, cultural anthropology, semiology, etc.

An institute which devotes itself to research of this kind should, like the Bohr Institute, be a place for meetings, observations and the distillation of experiments collected by the most fruitful individuals in this field from different theatres in every country. Taking into account the fact that the domain on which our attention is focussed is not a scientific one and not everything in it can be defined (indeed, many things must not be), we nevertheless try to determine our aims with all the precision and consequence proper to scientific research.
The actor who works here is already a professional for, not only his creative act but also the laws which govern it, become the object of his preoccupations. An institute for methodical research is not to be confused with a school that trains actors and whose job it is to "launch" them. Nor should this activity be confused with theatre (in the normal sense of the word) although the very essence of the research demands the elaboration of a performance and its confrontation with an audience. One cannot establish a method yet remain aloof from the creative act.

III

I am interested in the actor because he is a human being. This involves two principal points: firstly, my meeting with another person, the contact, the mutual feeling of comprehension and the impression created by the fact that we open ourselves to another being, that we try to understand him: in short, the surmounting of our solitude. Secondly, the attempt to understand oneself through the behaviour of another man, finding oneself in him. If the actor reproduces an act that I have taught him, this is a sort of "dressage". The result is a banal action from a methodical point of view, and in my heart of hearts I find it sterile for nothing has opened up before me. But if, in close collaboration, we reach the point where the actor, released from his daily resistances, profoundly reveals himself through a gesture, then I consider that from a methodical point of view the work has been effective. I shall then be personally enriched, for in that gesture a kind of human experience will have been revealed, something rather special that might be defined as a destiny, a human condition.

This applies to the relationship between the producer and a single actor, but if this concept is extended to the whole troupe, a new perspective opens up onto the limits of this collective life, onto the common ground of our convictions, our beliefs, our superstitions and the conditions of contemporary life.
If such a common ground exists, we will, in all sincerity, inevitably arrive at the confrontation between tradition and contemporaneity, myth and disbelief, the subconscious and the collective imagination.

I do not put on a play in order to teach others what I already know. It is after the production is completed and not before that I am wiser. Any method which does not itself reach out into the unknown is a bad method.

When I say that the action must engage the whole personality of the actor if his reaction is not to be lifeless, I am not talking of something "external" such as exaggerated gestures or tricks. What, then, do I mean? It is a question of the very essence of the actor's calling, of a reaction on his part allowing him to reveal one after the other the different layers of his personality, from the biological-instinctive source via the channel of consciousness and thought, to that summit which is so difficult to define and in which all becomes unity. This act of the total unveiling of one's being becomes a gift of the self which borders on the transgression of barriers and love. I call this a total act. If the actor performs in such a way, he becomes a kind of provocation for the spectator.

From a methodical point of view this is effective for it gives him a maximum of suggestive power on condition, of course, that he avoids chaos, hysteria, exaltation. It must be an objective act: that is to say articulated, disciplined. But above and beyond methodical efficacity, a new perspective also opens up for the spectator. The actor's accomplishment constitutes a transcendance of the half measures of daily life, of the internal conflict between body and soul, intellect and feelings, physiological pleasures and spiritual aspirations. For a moment the actor finds himself outside the semi-engagement and conflict which characterize us in our daily life. Did he do this for the spectator? The expression "for the spectator" implies a certain coquetry, a certain falseness, a bargaining with oneself. One should rather say "in relation to" the spectator or, perhaps, instead of him. It is precisely here that the provocation lies.

I am talking of the method, I am speaking of the surpassing of limits, of a confrontation, of a process of self-knowledge and, in a certain sense, of a therapy. Such a method must remain open – its very life depends on this condition – and is different for each individual. This is how it should be, for its intrinsic nature demands that it be individual.

Actor's Training (1959-1962)

The exercises in this chapter are the result of work and research during the years 1959–62. They were recorded by Eugenio Barba during the period he spent at the Theatre Laboratory and supplemented by my comments and those of our instructors who, under my guidance, directed the training.

During this time, I was searching for a positive technique or, in other words, a certain method of training capable of objectively giving the actor a creative skill that was rooted in his imagination and his personal associations. Certain elements from these exercises were retained in the training during the period that followed, but their aim has changed. All the exercises which merely constituted an answer to the question: "How can this be done?" were eliminated. The exercises have now become a pretext for working out a personal form of training. The actor must discover those resistances and obstacles which hinder him in his creative task. Thus the exercises become a means of overcoming these personal impediments. The actor no longer asks himself: "How can I do this?". Instead, he must know what **not** to do, what obstructs him. By a personal adaptation of the exercises, a solution must be found for the elimination of these obstacles which vary for each individual actor.

This is what I mean by **via negativa:** a process of elimination. The difference between the training of 1959–62 and the subsequent phase is most marked in the physical and vocal exercises. Most of the basic elements of the physical exercises have been retained, but they have been orientated towards a quest for contact: the receiving of stimuli from the exterior and reaction to these (the process of "give and take" mentioned elsewhere). The resonators are still used in the vocal exercises, but these are now set in action through various types of impulses and contact with the exterior.

In theory, there are no breathing exercises. I have explained my reasons for eliminating these in "The Techniques of the Actor" (page 207). According to each individual case, one discovers the difficulties in question, determining their cause and thereafter eradicating them. We do not work directly with respiration, but correct it indirectly by means of individual exercises which are almost always of a psycho-physical nature.

Jerzy Grotowski.

* * *

The training consists of exercises worked out by the actors or adopted from other systems. Even those exercises which are not the result of the actor's personal research have been developed and elaborated in order to satisfy the precise aims of the method. The terminology pertaining to the chosen exercises is then altered. Once the actors adopt a given exercise, they themselves establish a name for it on the basis of personal associations and ideas. One tends consciously to use a kind of professional jargon since this has a stimulating effect on the imagination.

The following is a rough outline of a day's training.

A. PHYSICAL EXERCISES

I – Warming up

1) Rhythmical walking while the arms and hands rotate.
2) Running on tiptoe. The body must feel a sensation of fluidity, flight, weightlessness. The impulse for the run comes from the shoulders.
3) Walk with knees bent, hands on hips.
4) Walk with knees bent, gripping the ankles.
5) Walk with the knees slightly bent, the hands touching the outside edges of the feet.
6) Walk with the knees slightly bent, holding the toes with one's fingers.

7) Walk with the legs stretched and rigid as though they were being pulled by imaginary strings held by the hands (the arms stretched out in front).

8) Starting in a curled up position, take short jumps forward, always landing in the original curled up position with the hands beside the feet.

Note: Even during these warming up exercises the actor must justify every detail of this training with a precise image, whether real or imaginary. The exercise is correctly executed only if the body does not oppose any resistance during the realisation of the image in question. The body should therefore appear weightless, as malleable as plasticine to the impulses, as hard as steel when acting as a support, capable even of conquering the law of gravity.

II – Exercises to loosen up the muscles and the vertebral column

1) "The cat". This exercise is based on the observation of a cat as it awakes and stretches itself. The subject lies stretched out face downwards, completely relaxed. The legs are apart and the arms at right angles to the body, palms towards the floor. The "cat" wakes up and draws the hands in towards the chest, keeping the elbows upwards, so that the palms of the hands form a basis for support. The hips are raised, while the legs "walk" on tiptoe towards the hands. Raise and stretch the left leg sideways, at the same time lifting and stretching the head. Replace the left leg on the ground, supported by the tips of the toes. Repeat the same movements with the right leg, the head still stretching upwards. Stretch the spine, placing the centre of gravity first in the centre of the spine, and then higher up towards the nape of the neck. Then turn over and fall onto the back, relaxing.

2) Imagine you have a metal band around the chest. Stretch it by means of a vigorous expansion of the trunk.

3) Handstand with the feet together against the wall. The legs slowly open as wide as possible.
4) Resting position. Squatting with the head dropped forward and the arms dangling between the knees.
5) Upright position, with the legs together and straight. Flex the trunk towards the ground until the head touches the knees.
6) Vigorous rotation of the trunk from the waist upwards.
7) Keeping the legs together, jump up onto a chair. The impulse for the jump does not come from the legs but from the trunk.
8) Total or partial splits.
9) Starting from an upright position, bend the body backwards to form a "bridge"until the hands touch the ground behind.
10) Lying position stretched out on one's back. Roll the whole body vigorously to left and right.
11) From a kneeling position, bend the body backwards into a "bridge" until the head touches the ground.
12) Jumps imitating those of a kangaroo.
13) Sit on the floor with the legs together and stretched out in front, the body erect. The hands, placed at the back of the neck, press the head forward and downwards until it touches the knees.
14) Walk on the hands and feet, with the chest and abdomen facing upwards.

Note: It is equally incorrect to perform this series of exercises in an inanimate way. **The exercise serves the research.** It is not merely automatic repetition or a form of muscular massage. For example, during the exercises one investigates the body's centre of gravity, the mechanism for the contraction and relaxation of the muscles, the function of the spine in the various violent movements, analysing any complicated developments and relating them to the repertory of every single joint and muscle. All this is individual and is the result of continual and total research. Only the exercises which "investigate" involve the entire organism of the actor and mobilise his hidden resources. The exercises which "repeat" give inferior results.

136

III – "Upside-down" exercises

Note: These exercises are positions rather than acrobatics and, in accordance with the rules of Hatha Yoga, they are performed at a very slow pace. One of the principal aims during their execution is the study of the changes which take place in the organism; namely, the study of the respiration, the rhythm of the heart, the laws of balance and the relationship between position and movement.

1) Headstand using the forehead and both hands as supports.
2) Headstand – Hatha Yoga position.
3) Headstand supported by the left (or right) shoulder, cheek and arm.
4) Headstand supported by the forearms.

IV – Flight

1) Squatting on the heels in a curled up position, hop and sway like a bird ready to take flight. The hands help the movement as wings.
2) Still hopping, raise yourself into an upright position, while the hands flap like wings in an effort to lift the body.
3) Take off in flight with successive forward movements somewhat similar to the action of swimming. While the body is carrying out these swimming movements, there is only one point of contact with the ground (e. g. the ball of one foot). Take swift leaps forward, still on the ball of one foot. Another method is as follows: recall to mind the flying sensation one experiences in dreams and spontaneously recreate this form of flight.
4) Land like a bird.

Note: Combine these exercises with others based on falls, somersaults, leaps, etc. One should aim at achieving a long flying-leap which begins like a bird taking off and finishes as it comes to land.

V – Leaps and somersaults

1) Forward somersaults using the hands as supports.
    a) Forward somersault, helping oneself up with one's hands.
    b) Forward somersault, without the use of the hands.
    c) Forward somersault, finishing up on one leg.
    d) Forward somersault with the hands behind the back.
    e) Forward somersault with one shoulder touching the ground for support.
2) Backward somersaults.
3) "Tiger" spring (diving forward). With or without a preparatory run, arms outstretched, spring over an obstacle into a somersault, landing on one shoulder. Get up in the same movement.
    a) High "tiger" spring.
    b) Long "tiger" spring.
4) "Tiger" spring followed immediately by a backward somersault.
5) Somersault with the body rigid like a marionette, yet as though there were a spring inside it.
6) "Tiger" spring performed simultaneously by two actors who cross one another in the air at different heights.
7) "Tiger" springs combined with somersaults in "battle" situations, using sticks or other weapons.

Note: Throughout these exercises, apart from the "research" factor and study of one's own organism, there is also an element of rhythm and dance. The exercises – especially in the case of the "battle" variations – are performed to the beat of a drum, tambourine or other object, so that both the performer of the exercise and he who beats out the rhythm improvise and provide a reciprocal stimulus. In the "battle" sequences, the physical reactions are accompanied by spontaneous and inarticulate cries. The actor must justify all these semi-acrobatic exercises with personal motivations, stressing the composition of the initial and final phases of the exercise.

VI – **Foot exercises**

1) Lie on the floor with the legs slightly raised. Do the following movements with the feet:
   a) Bending and stretching of the ankles, forwards and backwards.
   b) Bending and stretching of the ankles, sideways.
   c) Rotatory movements of the feet.
2) Standing position:
   a) Bend at the knees with arms outstretched, keeping the feet flat on the floor in the same spot all the time.
   b) Walk on the edges of the feet.
   c) Walk pigeon-toed (i. e. with toes turned inwards, heels well apart) on tiptoe.
   d) Walk on the heels.
   e) Bend the toes in towards the sole of the foot and then upwards in the opposite direction.
   f) Pick up small objects with the toes (a box of matches, a pencil, etc.).

VII – **Mime exercises concentrating mainly on the hands and legs**

VIII – **Studies in acting on any theme, performed while walking and running**

B. PLASTIC EXERCISES

I – **Elementary exercises**

Note: These exercises are based on Dalcroze and other classical European methods. Their fundamental principle is the study of opposite vectors. Particularly important is the study of vectors of opposite movements (e.g. the hand makes circular movements in one direction, the elbow in the opposite direction) and contrasting images (e.g. the hands accept, while the legs reject). In this way,

139

each exercise is subordinate to "research" and to the study of one's own means of expression, of their resistances and their common centres in the organism.

1) Walk rhythmically with arms stretched out to the side. Rotate the shoulders and arms, pushing the elbows back as far as possible. The hands rotate in the opposite direction to the shoulders and arms. The whole body reinforces these movements and, while rotating, the shoulders are raised absorbing the neck. Imagine you are a dolphin. Gradually increase the rhythm of the rotations, let the body grow in height, walking on the tips of the toes.

2) "Tug-of-war". An imaginary rope is stretched in front of you and is to be used to help you advance. It is not the arms and hands which pull the body, but the trunk which moves towards the hands. Heave yourself forward until the leg behind touches the ground with the knee. The body movement must be sharp and strong like the bows of a ship cleaving a huge wave.

3) Make a jump forward on the tips of the toes, bending the knees on landing. Return to a standing position with an elastic and energetic movement and repeat the same jump forward, still on tiptoe, followed by the knee-bend. The impulse comes from the thighs which act as the spring regulating the bending phase and the jump which follows. The arms are stretched out to the side and while one palm caresses, the other repels. One must have a sensation of being extremely light, soft and elastic like foam rubber.

4) Opposite rotatory movements. Standing position with the feet apart. Make four rotations with the head towards the right, then with the trunk towards the left, with the spine towards the right, with the hips towards the left, with the left leg towards the right, with the thigh to the left, with the ankle to the right, and so on with the right arm circling towards the left, the forearm towards the right and the hand itself towards the left. The entire body is involved, but the impulse comes from the base of the spine.

140

5) Stand with feet apart and arms stretched above the head, palms touching. Rotation of the trunk, bending towards the ground as far as possible. The arms accompany this double movement of circling and bending. Return to the initial position and, bending backwards, finish off the exercise in a "bridge".

6) Walking rhythmically. The first step is a normal one; on the second, bend at the knees until the buttocks touch the heels, keeping the trunk erect. Rise to a standing position in the same rhythm and repeat the same sequence of a normal step alternated with a knee-bend.

7) Improvisations with the hands. Touch, skim, feel, caress various objects, materials, textures. The entire body expresses these tactile sensations.

8) Games with one's own body. Give yourself a concrete task such as opposing one side of the body to the other. The right side is graceful, deft, beautiful, with movements that are attractive and harmonious. The left side jealously watches the right side, expressing in its movements its feelings of resentment and hate. It attacks the right side in order to avenge its inferiority, and tries to degrade and destroy it. The left side wins, and yet at the same time it is bound to lose, for without the right side it cannot survive, it cannot move. This is just one example. The body can easily be divided into opposing sections; for example, the upper versus the lower half. In the same way, single limbs can be opposed to one another – a hand versus a leg, one leg versus the other, the head versus a hand, etc. The important thing is to engage fully one's imagination which must give life and meaning not only to those parts of the body which are directly involved, but also to those which are not. For instance, during a fight between one hand and the other, the legs might express terror and the head astonishment.

9) Unexpected movements. Make a movement as, for instance, the rotation of both arms. This movement begins in one direction which, after a few seconds, proves to be the wrong one:

that is to say, the opposite to that intended. The direction is then changed, after a brief moment of immobility. The beginning of the movement must always be emphasized and then suddenly change – after a moment of immobility – to the correct movement. Another example: start walking slowly, as if with difficulty and effort. Suddenly, after standing still for a moment, start to run very lightly and gracefully.

II – Exercises in composition

Note: These exercises have been adapted according to the process of the formation of gesticulatory ideograms as in ancient and mediaeval theatre in Europe as well as African and oriental theatre. It is not, however, a question of seeking fixed ideograms as, for example, in the Peking Opera in which, in order to portray a particular flower, the actor makes a specific and unchangeable gesture inherited from centuries of tradition. New ideograms must constantly be sought and their composition appear immediate and spontaneous. The starting point for such gesticulatory forms is the stimulation of one's own imagination and the discovery in oneself of primitive human reactions. The final result is a living form possessing its own logic. These exercises in composition present unlimited possibilities. Here only a few of those which are suitable for further development will be dealt with.

1) The blossoming and withering of the body. Walk rhythmically. As in a plant, the sap rises, starting from the feet and spreading upwards through the entire body, reaching the arms which burst into blossom as indeed does the whole body. In the second phase, the limbs-branches wither and die one by one. Finish the exercise on the same rhythmic step with which it began.
2) Animal image. This does not consist in the literal and realistic imitation of a four-legged animal. One does not "act" an ani-

mal but attacks one's subconscious, creating an animal figure whose particular character expresses an aspect of the human condition. One must start from an association. Which animal does one associate with pity, cunning, wisdom? The association must not be banal, stereotyped – the lion representative of strength, the wolf of cunning, etc. It is also important to determine the animal's centre of vitality (the muzzle for the dog, the spinal cord for the cat, the belly for the cow, etc.).

3) By means of association with people, situations, memories, metamorphose yourself into a tree. The muscles react, expressing the personal association. To begin with, one concentrates these associations on one particular part of the body. As the reactions increase in intensity, the rest of the body is included. The vitality of this tree, its tensions, relaxations, micro-movements are nourished by the association.

4) The flower. The feet are the roots, the body is the stem and the hands represent the corolla. The whole body lives, trembles, vibrates with the imperious process of bursting into flower, guided by one's associations. Give "the flower" a logical signification, one which is at the same time sad, tragic and dangerous. "The flower" is separated from the process which created it and that part of it expressed through the hands is used as a rhetorical gesture in a dialogue.

5) Walk barefoot, imagining you are walking on different types of ground, surface, matter (soft, slippery, rough, smooth, wet, inflated, prickly, dry, on snow, on burning sand, at the water's edge, etc.). The feet are the centres of expressiveness, communicating their reactions to the rest of the body. Repeat the same exercise wearing shoes and try to retain the expressiveness of bare feet. The same exercise is next applied to the hands which feel, touch, caress specific materials and surfaces (still imaginary). Now make the hands and feet react simultaneously, often to opposite impulses.

6) Analogy with a new-born baby.
   a) Observe a new-born baby and compare its reactions to those of one's own body.

b) Search for any vestiges of infancy in one's own behaviour (e.g. someone smokes like a child sucking at its mother's breast).

c) Find those stimuli which reawaken in one the needs of infancy (e.g. a person who gives a sense of security, the desire to suck, the need for a feeling of warmth, interest in one's own body, a desire for consolation).

7) The study of different types of gait.

a) Type of gait determined by age, transferring the centre of the movement to different parts of the body. In infancy, the legs are the centre of movement; in the adolescent period, the shoulders; in manhood, the trunk; in maturity, the head; in old age, the legs again. Observe the changes in the vital rhythm. For the adolescent the world is slow in relation to his movements, whereas for the old man the world moves fast in relation to him. These are, of course, only two of the possible keys for interpretation.

b) Types of gait depending on different psychical dynamics (flegmatic, bellicose, nervous, sleepy, etc.).

c) Gaits as a means for unmasking those characteristics that one wishes to hide from others.

d) Different types of gait depending on physiological and pathological characteristics.

e) Parodies of other people's gaits. The essential thing here is to capture the motives and not the result of the way of walking. The unmasking is bound to be superficial if it does not contain an element of self-irony, if the fun made of others is not at one's own expense.

8) Choose an emotional impulse (such as crying) and transfer it to a particular part of the body – a foot, for example – which then has to give it expression. A concrete example of this is Eleonora Duse who, without using her face or arms, "kissed" with her whole body. Express two contrasting impulses with two different parts of the body: the hands laugh while the feet cry.

144

9) Catch the light with parts of the body. Animate these parts, creating forms, gestures, movements.
10) Moulding of the muscles: the shoulder cries like a face; the abdomen exults; a knee is greedy.

D. EXERCISES OF THE FACIAL MASK

These exercises are based on various suggestions made by Delsarte, particularly his division of each facial reaction into introversive and extroversive impulses. Every reaction can, in fact, be included in one of the following categories:

I) Movement creating contact with the external world (extroversive).
II) Movement which tends to draw attention from the external world in order to concentrate it on the subject (introversive).
III) Intermediate or neutral stages.

A close examination of the mechanism of these three types of reaction is very useful for the composition of a role. On the basis of these three types of reaction, Delsarte supplies a detailed and exact analysis of the human body's reactions and even those of parts of the body such as the eyebrows, eyelids, eyelashes, lips etc. Delsarte's interpretation of these three types of reactions is not, however, acceptable since it is bound to nineteenth century theatrical conventions. A purely personal interpretation must be made.

The reactions of the face correspond closely with the reactions of the entire body. This does not, however, exempt the actor from executing facial exercises. In this respect, in addition to Delsarte's prescriptions, the type of training for the facial musculature used by the actor from the classical Indian theatre, Kathakali, is appropriate and useful.

145

This training aims to control every muscle of the face, thus transcending stereotyped mimicry. It involves a consciousness and use of every single one of the actor's facial muscles. It is very important to be able to set in motion simultaneously, but at different rhythms, the various muscles of the face. For example, make the eyebrows quiver very fast while the cheek muscles tremble slowly, or the left side of the face react vivaciously while the right side is sluggish.

*   *   *

All the exercises described in this chapter must be performed without interruption, without pause for rest or private reactions. Even short rests must be incorporated as an integral part of the exercises, whose aim is not a muscular development or physical perfectionism, but a process of research leading to the annihilation of one's body's resistances.

146

TECHNIQUE OF THE VOICE

Carrying power

Special attention should be paid to the carrying power of the voice so that the spectator not only hears the voice of the actor perfectly, but is also penetrated by it as if it were stereophonic. The spectator must be surrounded by the actor's voice as if it came from every direction and not just the spot where the actor is standing. The very walls must speak with the voice of the actor. This concern for the voice's carrying power is further necessary in order to avoid vocal problems which may become serious.

The actor must exploit his voice in order to produce sounds and intonations that the spectator is incapable of reproducing or imitating.

The two conditions necessary for good vocal carrying power are:

a) The column of air carrying the sound must escape with force and without meeting obstacles (e.g. a closed larynx or insufficient opening of the jaws).
b) The sound must be amplified by the physiological resonators. All this is closely linked with correct respiration. If the actor only breathes with the chest or the abdomen, he cannot store up enough air, so he forces himself to economise it, closing the larynx and thus distorting the voice and eventually provoking vocal disorders. Through total (upper thoracic and abdominal) respiration, however, he can accumulate a more than sufficient quantity of air. For this it is vital that the air column does not meet any obstacles such as the closing of the larynx or the tendency to speak with the jaws only half open.

Respiration

Empiric observation reveals three types of respiration:

a) Upper thoracic or pectoral respiration, prevalent in Europe, especially amongst women.

b) Lower or abdominal respiration. The abdomen expands without the chest being used at all. This is the type of respiration usually taught in theatre schools.

c) Total (upper thoracic and abdominal) respiration, the abdominal phase being dominant. This is the most hygienic and functional type, and is found in children and animals.

Total respiration is the most effective for the actor. However, one must not be dogmatic about this. Every actor's breathing varies according to his physiological make-up, and whether or not he adopts total respiration should be dependent upon this. There also exists a certain natural difference between the respiratory possibilities of men and women. In women, correct respiration has a definite abdominal phase, although the upper thoracic element is slightly more developed than in men. The actor should practise different types of respiration since various positions and physical actions (acrobatics, for example) demand a form of respiration other than the total one.

It is necessary to accustom oneself to total respiration. That is, one must be able to control the functioning of the respiratory organs. It is well known that the different schools of yoga – including Hatha Yoga – demand the daily practice of respiratory techniques in order to control and exploit the biological function of breathing which has become automatic. Hence the need for a series of exercises to create an awareness of the respiratory process.

There are several methods of verifying whether respiration is total.

a) Lie on the ground or on any hard surface so that the vertebral column is quite straight. Place one hand on the chest and the other on the abdomen. While breathing in, one should feel the hand on the abdomen being raised first and then the one on the chest, all in one smooth, continuous movement. Care must be taken not to divide total respiration into two separate phases. The expansion of the chest and abdomen should be free of tension and the succession of the two phases should not be noticeable. Their concatenation must produce a sensation of slight swelling of the trunk. Subdivision of the phases can bring about inflammation of the vocal organs and even nervous disorders. At the beginning, the actor should practise under the guidance of an instructor.

b) Method adopted from Hatha Yoga. The vertebral column must be quite straight and for this it is necessary to lie on a hard surface. Block one nostril with a finger and breathe in through the other. When breathing out do the contrary: block the nostril through which you breathed in before and breathe out through the one which was blocked at the beginning. The three phases succeed one another in the following rhythm:

Inspiration:	4 seconds
Hold the breath:	12 seconds
Expiration:	8 seconds

c) The method which follows, taken from the classical Chinese theatre, is basically the most effective and can be used in any position whereas the two previous ones necessitate lying down. While standing, place the hands on the two lowest ribs. Inspiration must give an impression of beginning in the very spot where the hands are placed (therefore pushing them outwards) and, continuing through the thorax, produce a sensation that the air column reaches right up to the head. (This means that, when breathing in, the abdomen and lower ribs dilate first, followed, in smooth succession, by the chest). The abdominal wall is then contracted while the ribs remain expanded, thus forming a base for the air stored up and preventing it from escaping with the first words uttered. The abdominal wall (contracting inwards) pulls in the opposite direction to the muscles which expand the lower ribs (contracting outwards), keeping them thus for as long as possible during expiration.

149

(A common error is the compression of the abdominal muscles before total inspiration is completed, resulting in upper thoracic breathing only). Expiration takes place inversely: from the head, through the thorax, to the spot where the palms of the hands are placed. Care must be taken not to compress the indrawn air too much and – as already mentioned – the whole process must take place smoothly: in other words, without any division between the abdominal and upper thoracic phases. An exercise such as this is not intended to teach respiration for respiration's sake, but prepares for a respiration that will "carry" the voice. It also teaches how to establish a base (the abdominal wall) which, by contracting, allows the easy and vigorous emission of the air and thus the voice.

During total respiration do not store up or compress too much air. The actor must acquire the greatest possible independence with regard to organic respiration, avoiding a form of respiration that demands pauses which might interfere with the recitation of a text. A good actor breathes in silently and quickly. He breathes at the place in the text (whether prose or poetry) he has established as a logical pause. This is functional since it saves time and avoids superfluous pauses; it is necessary since it lays down the rhythm of the text.

The actor must always know when to breathe. For example, in a scene with a fast rhythm, he must breathe before the end of his companion's last words in order to be ready to speak as soon as his companion has finished. On the other hand, if he breathes at the end of the latter's speech, there will be a brief silence in the midst of the dialogue, creating a "hole" in the rhythm.

Exercises for rapid and silent inspiration:

a) Standing with his hands on his hips, the actor quickly and quietly takes in a large mouthful of air with his lips and teeth before uttering a few words.

150

b) Take a series of short silent breaths, gradually increasing in speed. Breathe out normally.

Do not overdo the respiratory exercises. Breathing is an organic and spontaneous process and the exercises are not intended to submit it to a strict control but to correct any anomalies, nevertheless retaining its spontaneity. In order to do this, the respiratory and vocal exercises must be combined and the respiration corrected where necessary. If, during the execution of his score, the actor concentrates on his breathing, consciously forcing himself to control it and yet unable to rid himself of this thought, then it is true to say that the respiratory exercises have been wrongly performed.

Opening of the larynx

Take special care to open the larynx when speaking and breathing. The closing of the larynx prevents the effective emission of the air, thus denying the actor the correct use of his voice.

One can tell that the larynx is closed if:
a) The voice is flat;
b) One has a concrete sensation of the larynx in the throat;
c) When breathing in, a slight noise be heard;
d) The Adam's apple moves upwards (for example, when swallowing, the larynx is closed and the Adam's apple is raised);
e) The muscles at the back of the neck are contracted;
f) The muscles under the chin are contracted (one can check this by placing the thumb under the chin and the index finger below the lower lip);
g) The lower jaw is too far forward or too far back.

The larynx is always open if one experiences the sensation of having plenty of room in the back of the mouth (as when yawning).

151

The larynx is always open if one experiences the sensation of having plenty of room in the back of the mouth (as when yawning).

The closing of the larynx is often the result of bad habits acquired in theatre schools. The most frequent examples of this are the following:

a) The pupil performs exercises in diction before he has learnt to control his respiration. He attempts to obtain an effective carrying power with the help of diction alone and with the intention of economising the indrawn air, closes the larynx.

b) The pupil is often asked to breathe in and then count aloud. The higher he counts, the more he is congratulated on his ability to economise his breath. This is an unforgivable mistake because, in order to succeed, the pupil closes his larynx, thus deteriorating his carrying power. On the contrary, it is essential to breathe in very deeply and **not** try to economise the air. Every word must be enveloped, as though saturated with air, especially the vowels. Care must be taken, however, not to be left without air between words.

c) Faulty respiration which may appear to be correct. Often the pupil dilates the abdomen as though he were breathing in, but in actual fact only upper thoracic breathing occurs.

Basic exercise to open the larynx (prescribed by the Chinese doctor Ling):

Stand with the upper part of the body, including the head, bent slightly forward. The lower jaw, fully relaxed, rests on the thumb, while the index finger rests lightly below the lower lip to prevent the lower jaw from dropping. Raise the upper jaw and the eyebrows, at the same time wrinkling the forehead so that you have a sensation that the temples are being stretched as in a yawn, while contracting slightly the muscles of the top and back of the head and the back part of the neck. Finally, let the voice come out. Throughout the whole exercise check that the muscles beneath the chin are relaxed and soft: the thumb supporting the chin must meet no resistance whatever. The errors one usually comes across during this exercise are: the contraction of the muscles of the chin and front part of the neck, the incorrect position of the lower jaw (placed too far back), the relaxing of the head muscles and the dropping of the lower jaw instead of the lifting of the upper jaw.

Resonators

The task of the physiological resonators is to amplify the carrying power of the sound emitted. Their function is to compress the column of air into the particular part of the body selected as an amplifier for the voice. Subjectively one has the impression that one is speaking with the part of the body in question – the head, for example, if using the upper resonator[1].

In reality, there is an almost infinite number of resonators, depending on the control the actor has over his own physical instrument. We shall limit ourselves here to mentioning just a few.

a) The upper or head resonator which is the one most employed in European theatre. Technically, it functions through the pressure of the flow of air into the front part of the head. One can easily become aware of this resonator by placing the

---

(1) The term "resonator" is purely conventional. From a scientific point of view it has not been proved that the subjective pressure of the indrawn air into a determined part of the body (thus creating an external vibration of the spot) causes this area to function objectively as a resonator. Nevertheless, it is a fact that this subjective pressure, together with its obvious symptom (vibration), modifies the voice and its carrying power.

hand on the upper part of the forehead and enunciating the consonant "m", when one should be able to feel a definite vibration. Generally speaking, the upper resonator comes into use when speaking in a high register. Subjectively one can feel the air column passing through, being compressed and finally hitting the upper part of the head. When using this resonator one must have the sensation that the mouth is situated at the top of the head.

b) The chest resonator, known in Europe although rarely used consciously. It functions when one speaks in a low register. To check whether it is in action, place a hand on the chest which should vibrate. To use it, speak as though the mouth were situated in the chest.

c) The nasal resonator which is also known in Europe. This functions automatically when the consonant "n" is pronounced. It has been unjustly abolished by most theatre schools. It can be exploited to characterize certain parts or even a whole role.

d) The laryngeal resonator, used in oriental and African theatre. The sound produced recalls the roaring of wild animals. It is also characteristic of some negro singers of jazz (e. g. Armstrong).

e) The occipital resonator. This can be attained by speaking in a very high register. One projects the flow of air towards the upper resonator and, while speaking in a continually mounting register, the flow of air is then directed towards the occiput. During training, one can reach this resonator by producing a high pitched mewing sound. This resonator is commonly used in classical Chinese theatre.

f) In addition, there exists a series of resonators which actors often use unconsciously. For example, in so-called "intimate" acting, the maxillary resonator (in the back of the jaws) comes into use. Other resonators are to be found in the abdomen, and in the central and lower parts of the spine.

g) The most fruitful possibility lies in the use of the entire body as a resonator. This is obtained by using simultaneously the head and chest resonators. Technically, one must concentrate one's attention on the resonator which is not automatically in use at the moment in which one speaks. For example, when speaking in a high register, one normally uses the head resonator. One must therefore concentrate on exploiting simultaneously the chest resonator. In this case "concentrate" means to compress the air column into the inactive resonator. The opposite is necessary when speaking in a low register. Normally the chest resonator is in use, so one must concentrate on the head resonator. This resonator which engages the whole body can be defined as a total resonator.

Interesting effects can be obtained by simultaneously combining two resonators. The simultaneous use of the occipital and laryngeal resonators, for example, produces the vocal effects achieved by Yma Sumac in her renowned Peruvian songs. In some cases one can combine two resonators, making one of them function as a "solo" and the other as the "accompaniment". For instance, the maxillary resonator may give the "solo" while a uniform "accompaniment" is provided by the chest resonator.

Voice base

The use of any resonator presupposes the existence of an air column which, in order to be compressed, must have a base. The actor must learn consciously to find within himself a base for this column of air. This base can be acquired in the following ways:

a) By the expansion and contraction of the abdominal wall. This

155

method is often used by European actors, even though many of them are unaware of the real motive behind the muscular dilation. Opera singers often reinforce this base by crossing their hands on the abdomen and, pretending to hold a handkerchief, compressing the lower ribs with the forearms.

b) By the method used in classical Chinese theatre. The actor binds his waist with a broad belt, tightly fastened. When he breathes totally (abdominal and upper thoracic respiration), this belt compresses the muscles of the abdomen thus forming a base for the air column.

c) After breathing in totally (abdominal and upper thoracic breathing), the muscles of the belly are compressed, automatically forcing the air upwards. The lower ribs are pushed outwards and in this way a base is obtained for the air column. As already mentioned, a common error is that of compressing the abdominal muscles before the process of total respiration is completed (the result being upper thoracic breathing only).

Here too, it is important not to store up too much air during the contraction of the abdominal muscles as this causes the larynx to close. If the abdominal muscles are not contracted sufficiently slowly, a feeling of giddiness is experienced.
There are many more methods for creating a base for the air column. The actor must master many of these in order to be able to alternate them according to the role and the circumstances.

Placing the voice

There are two different ways of placing the voice, one for actors and another for singers, since their tasks are quite distinct. Many opera singers – even excellent ones – are incapable of giving a long speech without tiring their voice and therefore running the risk of becoming hoarse simply because their voice is placed for

156

Spatial solutions in the Theatre Laboratory. In this respect a very important role has been played by the architect Jerzy Gurawski, who is also the author of most of the projects presented here.

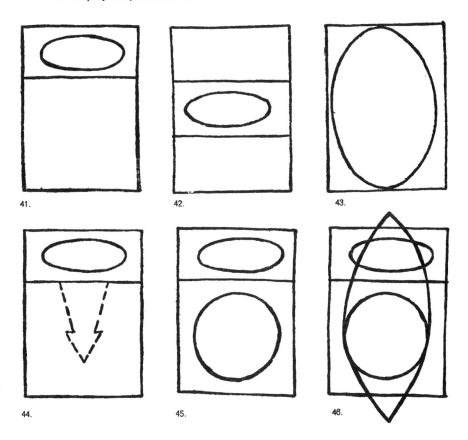

41. Italian stage. The actors are separated from the audience and always act within the same fixed area.

42. Theatre in the round (central stage). Although the position of the stage changes, the barrier between actor and spectator remains.

43. Theatre Laboratory. Actors and spectators are no longer separated. The whole room becomes the stage and, at the same time, the place for the spectators.

44. In the period of theatre reform at the beginning of our century, attempts were made (by Meyerhold, Piscator and others) to bring the actors down from time to time among the audience. The stage is still, however, the centre of the action.

45. The spectators are considered a unity of potential participants. The actors address them or may occasionally even be placed in the midst of them.

46. Theatre Laboratory. Here the producer always keeps in mind that he has two "ensembles" to direct: the actors and the spectators. The performance results from an integration of these two "ensembles".

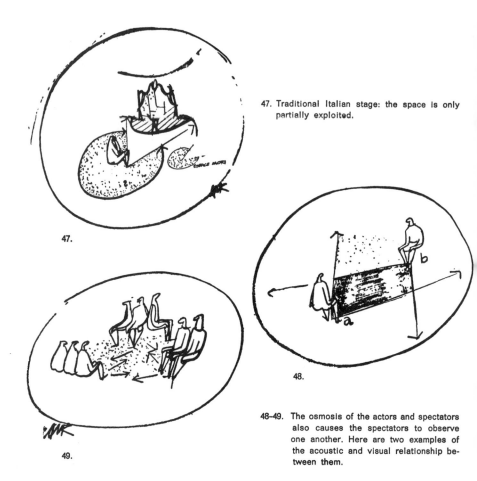

47. Traditional Italian stage: the space is only partially exploited.

47.

48.

48–49. The osmosis of the actors and spectators also causes the spectators to observe one another. Here are two examples of the acoustic and visual relationship between them.

49.

50. Relationship between the actors (in black) and the spectators. The latter are integrated in the scenic action and are considered as specific elements of the performance.

Spectators.

Actors.

50.

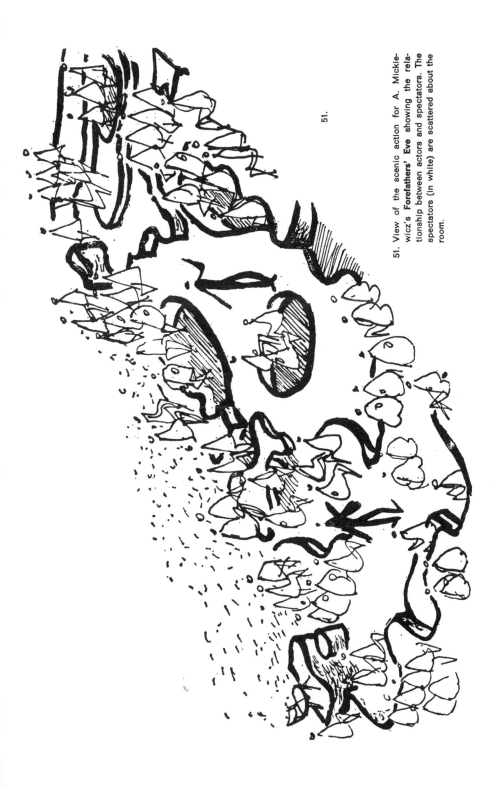

51.

51. View of the scenic action for A. Mickiewicz's **Forefathers' Eve** showing the relationship between actors and spectators. The spectators (in white) are scattered about the room.

The conquest of space in the Theatre Laboratory, beginning with the Italian stage and ending
with the full exploitation of the whole room even among the spectators.
Black areas: actors' place of action.
White areas: spectators.

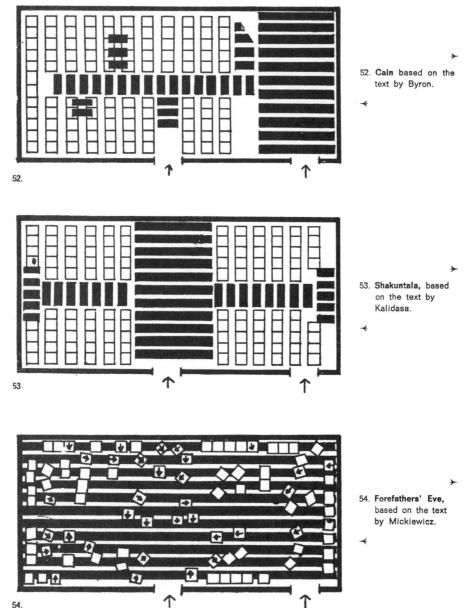

52.

52. **Cain** based on the
text by Byron.

53.

53. **Shakuntala,** based
on the text by
Kalidasa.

54.

54. **Forefathers' Eve,**
based on the text
by Mickiewicz.

,KAIN'

55.

56.

57.

161

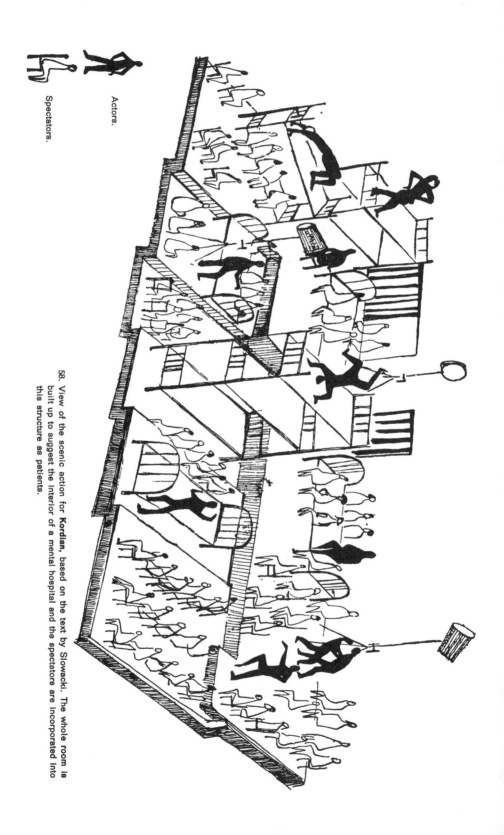

Actors.

Spectators.

58. View of the scenic action for **Kordian,** based on the text by Slowacki. The whole room is built up to suggest the interior of a mental hospital and the spectators are incorporated into this structure as patients.

59. Diagram showing the movement and areas of action in **Akropolis,** based on the text by Wyspianski.

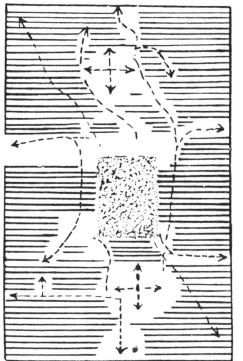

Central "mansion" where pipes are assembled and into which at the end the actors disappear.

Spectators.

Actors.

59.

60.

61.

Akropolis
60. The room at the beginning of the performance.
61. The room at the end of the performance.

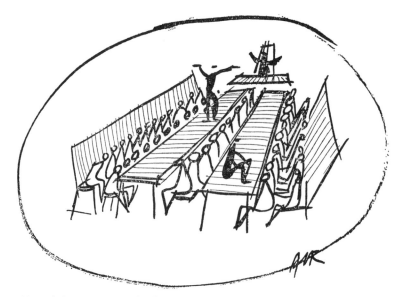

62. View of the scenic action for **Dr Faustus** based on Marlowe's text. One hour before his death, Faustus offers a last supper to his friends (the spectators).

63. View of the scenic action for **The Constant Prince** based on the text by Calderon-Slowacki. The spectators look down on a forbidden act, their positioning suggesting a bull-ring or an operating theatre.

singing and not for speaking. Theatre schools often make the mistake of teaching the future actor to place his voice for singing. The reason for this is often that the teachers are ex-opera singers and that frequently a musical instrument (piano) is used to accompany the vocal exercises.

Organic exercises

Previous observations which warn against depriving the actor of his organic respiration are also valid for the resonators, the opening of the larynx and the voice base. The aim of the exercises is to make the actor aware of his potential diapason. It is essential for him spontaneously and almost subconsciously to exploit these possibilities while executing the score of his role.

It often happens that the actor who performs his exercises badly, controls his voice, "listening to himself". This blocks the organic process and can give rise to a series of muscular tensions which, in their turn, prevent the correct emission of the voice (e. g. the partial closing of the larynx). A vicious circle is created: in the desire to use his voice correctly, the actor listens to himself; but by so doing, the whole vocal process is blocked and the correct emission of the voice becomes impossible. To avoid this, the actor must learn to control his own voice, listening to it not from within himself but from the outside. With this aim in view, an effective exercise is to utter a sound, directing it against a wall and listening to its echo. One does not listen passively to the echo, however, but consciously shapes it by moving nearer or farther from the wall, guiding it higher up or lower down at will and changing resonators, timbre, intonation.

In order to exploit organically one's respiratory and vocal apparatus according to the multiple demands of the role, individual research must be carried out. One must determine which images and associations produce, in a certain actor, the "opening" of the vocal apparatus (resonators, larynx, etc.).

165

For example, in some actors, the upper (head) resonator is automatically set in action when, while speaking, they direct the voice towards the ceiling with the hands, literally pushing the voice upwards. Similarly, one of the lower resonators may be set in motion by letting the hands direct the voice towards the ground.

The actor must always aim at spontaneous vocal reactions rather than ones which are coldly calculated. The following exercises are helpful in this respect:

a) Use the voice to create around oneself a circle of "hard" or "soft" air; with the voice build a bell which becomes successively larger and smaller; send a sound through a wide tunnel, then a narrow tunnel, etc.

b) Vocal actions against objects: use your voice to make a hole in the wall, to overturn a chair, to put out a candle, to make a picture fall from the wall, to caress, to push, to wrap up an object, to sweep the floor; use the voice as if it were an axe, a hand, a hammer, a pair of scissors, etc.

Vocal imagination

Apart from the conscious and hygienic exploitation of the vocal apparatus, there are two further means of increasing its possibilities:

a) The actor must learn to enrich his vocal faculties by uttering unusual sounds. An extremely helpful exercise in this respect consists in the imitation of natural sounds and mechanical noises: the dripping of water, the twittering of birds, the humming of a motor, etc. First imitate these sounds. Then fit them into a spoken text in such a way as to awaken the association of the sound you wish to convey ("colouring" the words).

b) The actor should develop the ability to speak in registers that are not his natural ones – i. e. higher or lower than normal. This does not merely mean methodically and continuously raising or lowering the voice to inhabitual registers but, in specific cases, operating artificially with unnatural registers without in any way hiding their artificiality. Another useful way of artificially attaining other registers is the parodied imitation of the voices of women, children, old people, etc. But the actor must never force himself methodically to lower his natural register in order to achieve, for example, a "virile" voice. This tendency is particularly harmful, provoking inflammation of the throat and even nervous disorders.

Vocal emploi

If the actor suffers from a slight vocal defect that cannot be eradicated, instead of forcing himself to conceal it, he should exploit it in different ways according to the roles he plays.

Diction

The basic rule for good diction is to expire the vowels and "chew" the consonants.

Do not pronounce letters over-distinctly. Often, instead of pronouncing a word as an entity, the actor splits it up according to the letters which compose it. This takes the life away from the word giving it the same characteristics of pronunciation as a foreign language learnt from a book. There is a fundamental difference between the written and the spoken word, the written word being only an approximation. Diction is a means of expression. The multiplicity of types of diction existing in life should also be found on the stage. Restriction to one single type of diction signifies an impoverishment of sound effects and con-

167

stitutes a refusal to make use of all the means at one's disposal – rather as if one were to compel all the actors to wear the same costume. Just as in life there is no one type of diction but innumerable ones depending on the age, health, character and psychosomatic structure of the particular individual, in the same way there can be no single form of scenic diction in the theatre. The actor must underline, parody and exteriorize the interior motives and psychical phases of the character he is playing by modifying his pronunciation or using a new type of diction. This also entails modification of the rhythm of respiration.

On stage, in general, the diction is characterized by a precise and monotonous pronunciation which, apart from being dull from an artistic point of view, also tends towards affectation. Taking as a basis the different types of diction to be observed in everyday life, depending on the physical and psychological peculiarities of the individual, the actor should aim at other types of artificial diction which help him to characterize, parody and unmask the role.

Every role necessitates a different type of diction and, even within the framework of the same role, the possibilities offered by changes in diction according to circumstances and situations must be exploited to the full.
Here are a few exercises with this in view:

a) Parody the diction of your own acquaintances.
b) Through diction alone, portray various characters (a miser, a parvenu, a glutton, a pious man, etc.).
c) Characterize through diction certain psychosomatic particularities (lack of teeth, a weak heart, neurasthenia, etc.).

The tendency to lay too much stress on consonants is erroneous. It is the vowels that should be stressed. Over-emphasis of the consonants causes the larynx to close. When, in practising diction, it is necessary to stress the consonants, the vowels should also be stressed proportionately. Every sentence should be emitted like a long respiratory wave which prevents the larynx from closing. Only when whispering is stress laid on the consonants which may, in this case, be emphasized.

Exercises in diction should never be practised on the text used in the performance in order to avoid distorting its interpretation. The best training in diction is obtained in one's private life. The actor must pay continual attention to his pronunciation, even outside the environment of his work. Another effective exercise for diction is to read a sentence very slowly, repeating it again and again, faster each time, without cutting short the vowels.

Exercises in rhythm control can be performed with the help of a metronome or one's own pulse. The same speed should be kept up right to the end. Do not speed up after the caesura in poetry or at the end of the sentence in prose.

Even when shouting or producing a very high tone, the actor always retains a reserve which allows him to increase the volume if necessary. Otherwise, the strain he puts on his voice will be noticeable.

The actor must never learn his part aloud. This automatically leads to an interpretational "petrification". Similarly, one must not recite one's part for fun in private life or amuse oneself with the props from the performance. Quite apart from being a lack of respect towards one's craft, it leads immediately to banality without the actor even realizing it. During rehearsals, the actor should be aware of the acoustic possibilities of the room in which he is acting in order to discover effects (echoes, sharp or muffled resonances, etc.) that he can put to conscious use, incorporating them into the structure of his role.

Pauses

It is important not to abuse pauses. The pause, as a means of expression, achieves its aim on these conditions:

a) Its parsimonious use, only where it adds expressivity.
b) The elimination of every pause which does not have an artistic function and is not dependent on the structure of the role (resulting from personal fatigue, natural prolixity, etc.).
c) The shortening of respiratory pauses which must always be rapid and smooth. It is advisable to make these coincide with the logical pauses.
d) Priority being given to the "artificial" or "false" pauses created by an interval. By interval is meant the transition from one tone of voice to another. The actor must always practise the short intervals which are far more difficult than the long ones.

Exploitation of errors

The actor must have the presence of mind rapidly to insert into the structure of the role any mistakes (in diction or movement) involuntarily committed during the performance. Instead of stopping or beginning again, he must continue, exploiting the error as an effect. For example, if an actor pronounces a word wrongly, he should not correct himself but repeat the mistaken pronunciation in other words in other passages so that the spectator understands it as an effect within the structure of the role. This technique naturally demands a command of one's reflexes and also a quality of improvisation.

Technique of pronunciation

There is no essential difference between the recitation of poetry

170

and prose. In both cases it is a question of rhythm, phrasing and logical accents.

In prose, the rhythm has to be discovered, or rather deciphered: one has to feel the specific rhythm of the text. A good actor is capable of rhythmically reading even a telephone directory. Rhythm is not synonymous with monotony or uniform prosody, but with pulsation, variation, sudden change. After determining various logical accents in the text according to the general plan of interpretation, one must then impose a rhythm which coincides with these accents. However, even in prose, one should not favour the rhythm to the detriment of a formal logic or, in the other extreme, neglect the rhythm in order to concentrate exclusively on the logical sense of the text. Nor should the rhythm of the text be chopped up or the logical accent be emphasized with pauses. The logical accent of a sentence must not be isolated: it represents the culminating point of a rhythmic flow produced by a single respiratory and melodic wave. It often happens that the logical accent is placed on two different words – perhaps even well apart from one another – in the same sentence.

The ability to handle sentences is important and necessary in acting. The sentence is an integral unit, emotional and logical, that can be sustained by a single expiratory and melodic wave. It is a whirlwind concentrated on an epicentrum formed by the logical accent or accents. The vowels of this epicentrum should not be shortened but rather prolonged slightly in order to give them a special value, taking good care not to break up the unity of the sentence with unjustified pauses. Exceptions can of course be made to this rule if one aims at a specific formal effect: in which case the epicentrum can be curtailed and the sentences broken up.

In poetry too, the sentence must be considered as a logical and emotional entity to be pronounced in one single respiratory wave. Several lines (one and a half, two or more) often constitute the sentence. Here the rhythm of every line must be established without resorting to monotonous means. The distinctive quality of the line must be retained, using several means and not just one, such as a tonic accent or a pause between lines.

There are innumerable ways of protecting the rhythm of each line. One can place a comma or a full stop at the end of one line, at the end of another make the logical accent fall on the last word, and use an interval (change of tone) at the end of a third, justifying it from the point of view of the interpretation.

The necessity of fixing the respiratory pauses exists in prose as in poetry. These should not be close together as this can cause breathlessness. If, on the other hand, they are too far apart and the actor tries to make his breath last out, the larynx will close. One can violate all the rules mentioned here provided this transgression is intentional and aims at a formal effect.

Other formal elements can also be employed:
a) Acceleration or slowing down of a sentence's rhythm.
b) Sudden changes in rhythm.
c) Unconcealed inspiration before the words which bear the sentence's logical accent.
d) Illogical inspiration: i.e. at a place in the sentence where breathing would not normally take place.

* * *

Every actor – even one who is technically skilled – undergoes some form of vocal crisis after a period of several years. This is due to age which changes the physical structure of the body, demanding a new adaptation of the technique. The actor who wants to avoid stagnation must periodically begin all over again, learning breathing, pronunciation and the use of his resonators. He must rediscover his voice.

Actor's Training (1966)

The following are notes by Franz Marijnen of the "Institut des Arts Spectaculaires" (INSAS) in Brussels during a course given by Jerzy Grotowski and his collaborator, Ryszard Cieslak, in 1966. On comparing the exercises with those of the 1959–62 period, a definite change is noticeable in the orientation and the object of the training, resulting from the work of the last few years. The fundamental principles of Grotowski's present via negativa in the exercises are described in the chapters "Towards a Poor Theatre" (p. 15), "The Actor's Technique" (p. 205) and in the closing speech from the Skara Seminar (p. 225). Translation: Vita Pedersen.

In his introduction, Grotowski mentions that contact between the audience and the actor is vital in the theatre. With this in mind he starts his lessons with the motto: "The essence of theatre is the actor, his actions and what he can achieve".

His lecture scheme and the various exercises are based on many years of experience and on scientific and methodical research into the techniques of the actor and his physical presence on the stage.

Vocal exercises

To begin with, Grotowski makes some remarks about the attitude to be adopted towards one's work. He demands absolute silence from all who are present in the room, both actors and audience. Laughter must be restrained even though at first the exercises may resemble something from a circus performance. Those who are not familiar with his method may receive this impression, but it is quickly expelled once one has attended a few lessons and seen the results achieved. The audience – in this case the people who do not take an active part in the exercises – must be "invisible and inaudible" to the pupils.

Stimulation of the voice

Each pupil chooses a text and is free to recite, sing or even shout it out. This exercise is performed in unison. In the meantime, Grotowski walks around amongst the pupils, sometimes feeling their chests, backs, heads or abdomens while they are speaking. Nothing escapes his notice.

After this exercise, he picks out four student actors. The others go back to their places in absolute silence, from where they are to watch the progress of their fellow students.

Grotowski places a student in the centre

- The pupil recites a text at will, his voice gradually increasing in volume.
- The words must resound against the ceiling as though the upper part of the skull were talking. The head must not be tilted back as this causes the larynx to close. Through the echo, the ceiling becomes the partner in the dialogue which takes the form of questions and answers. During the exercise Grotowski leads the pupil by the arm round the room.
- Then begins a conversation with the wall, also improvised. Here it becomes evident that the echo is the answer. The whole body must respond to the echo. The voice originates in and issues from the chest.
- Next the voice is placed in the belly. In this way a conversation is held with the floor. Position of the body: "Like a fat, heavy cow".

Note: Grotowski points out that during all these exercises thought must be excluded. The pupils are to speak the text without thinking and without a pause. Grotowski therefore interrupts every time he notices that the pupil is thinking during the exercises.

The whole cycle of exercises is performed, using in succession:
- The head voice (towards the ceiling)
- The mouth voice (as if speaking to the air in front of the actor)
- The occipital voice (towards the ceiling behind the actor)
- The chest voice (projected in front of the actor)
- The belly voice (towards the floor)

176

- The voice issuing from:
  a) the shoulder blades (towards the ceiling behind the actor)
  b) the small of the back (towards the wall behind the actor)
  c) the lumbar region (towards the floor, the wall and the room behind him)

Grotowski does not let the actor off lightly. While the latter is speaking, he moves around him stimulating and "kneading" certain parts of the pupil's body, thus releasing living impulses which automatically carry the voice.

The rhythm of the exercises is very fast. The whole body must be engaged in the exercises – even in the vocal ones.

One relaxation exercise consists of an improvised conversation with the wall, completely free of all tension. The pupil must constantly be aware that the echo is caught.

It is remarkable how Cieslak – Grotowski's main actor and closest collaborator – who must have performed and watched the exercises innumerable times follows the progress of the pupils with the greatest interest and attention.

"TIGER" exercise

This exercise is obviously intended to make the pupil let himself go completely and, at the same time, set the guttural resonator in action. Grotowski participates in the exercise himself. He plays the tiger attacking his prey. The pupil (the prey) reacts, roaring like a tiger (c. f. Armstrong's vocal improvisations). It is not only a question of roaring.

The sounds must be based on the text, the continuity of which is important in this kind of exercise.

Grotowski: "Come closer...Text...Shout... I am the tiger, not you ,... I am going to eat you ...". In this way he goads the pupil on to enter fully into the game. It is remarkable how the pupils are carried away by the exercise. By now all timidity has vanished.

177

The only obstacle is the lack of a familiar text, for words do not come easily while improvising.

Suddenly Grotowski interrupts the exercise (unnoticed by some of the pupils, so totally engaged are they in the exercise) and asks the pupil to sing a song. This is apparently meant to relax the voice. Grotowski considers such vocal relaxation to be of the greatest importance, especially for those pupils who are doing this kind of exercise for the first time. The vocal organs are not yet accustomed to being used in this way.

Grotowski's pedagogical strength is shown by the fact that the pupils are difficult to restrain after an exercise. They pay no attention to the audience which is itself remarkably engaged in the whole process.

"KING-KING" Exercise

The essence of this exercise is the repeated calling out of the word **"King"** on a very high note and in a quick tempo, with a whole series of variations ranging from very low to very high notes. Finally the sound issues from the occiput which at this moment **is** the mouth. Grotowski obtains the most amazing results by improvising around this word at a successively higher pitch.

After about five minutes, the pupil, under the pushing guidance of Grotowski, attains a height in the vocal scale that appears to be quite new to him. We noticed many surprised faces amongst fellow-pupils . . .

"LA-LA" Exercise

The exercise starts with the pupil walking around and singing **"La-la-la"**.

Grotowski then lies down on the floor beside the pupil. The **"La-la"** is now repeated against the ceiling, the wall and the floor, alternating between the head, belly and chest voice. Grotowski massages the pupil's belly to loosen up and stimulate the resonator situated there.

After this exercise the pupil remains on the floor for some moments, completely relaxed.

Note: The result is remarkable. Even after the first lesson the voice of the pupil in question reaches intonations and ranges that one would never have guessed he possessed.

*　　　*　　　*

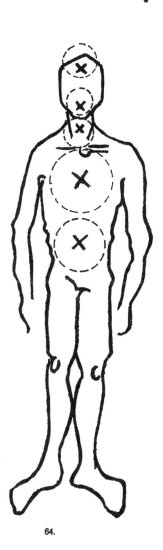

64.

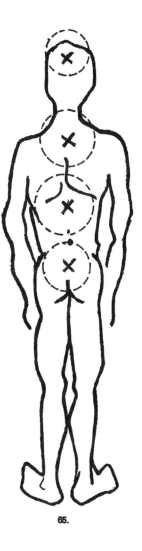

65.

64–65 Resonators.

Grotowski starts again with the same cycle of exercises as for the first pupil.

Stimulation of vocal impulses from the different resonators:
- The head voice (towards the ceiling)
- The mouth voice (as if speaking to the air in front of the actor)
- The occipital voice (towards the ceiling behind the actor)
- The chest voice (projected in front of the actor)
- The belly voice (towards the floor)
- The voice issuing from:
     a) the shoulder blades (towards the ceiling behind the actor)
     b) the small of the back (towards the wall behind the actor)
     c) the lumbar region (towards the floor, the wall and the room behind him)

The centres and resonators to be loosened in the back are indicated in the diagram 64–65 by an "x".

Next Exercise
The mewing of a cat with the widest range of:
a) Intonation
b) Nuances
c) Pitch
Suddenly Grotowski returns to the normal recitation of a text.

TIGER
Voice expressions in the form of a tiger's roar. There are already visible signs of progress in comparison with the previous pupil. The vocal exercises are now accompained by prowling, rolling and clawing movements. Grotowski has doubtless learnt from experience that the pupils need these associations in order to be able to surrender themselves fully to the exercise.

SOUNDS
The uttering of all possible kinds of inarticulate sounds in the most varied intonations attainable by the pupil. It is as though the pupil were opening the cage which enclosed, in latent form, his flora and fauna.

The tempo of these exercises is amazing. So too are the results in certain respects, for this pupil also attains a breadth of diapason which, he asserts afterwards, he has never before reached. He says this comes automatically and the results are due to the cycle of exercises and to the close co-operation. Also, the sincerity with which the exercises are performed and the sympathy of the others play a part that must not be underestimated.

Next Exercise
The actor lies outstretched on the ground in a relaxed position. Grotowski appeals to his imagination, yet encouraging him to think as little as possible. Reactions must not be sought. If they are not spontaneous they are of no use.
Grotowski indicates with the palm of his hand the places on the pupil's body that are warmed by the sun. In the meantime the pupil sings quietly. After some time the voice changes, the power and intensity of the song altering according to the parts of the body that Grotowski touches.

*   *   *

During the interval the actors are not allowed to speak amongst themselves and above all not to whisper. Later on Grotowski explains the reasons for this. The audience must remain as quiet as possible.
The approximate duration of the exercises for each pupil is thirty minutes.

A third pupil is asked to perform the same vocal exercises as the previous ones.
Here, however, Grotowski introduces a new element into the exercises: a form of yoga headstand. The actor has to recite a text and sing a song while standing on his head. A relaxation exercise follows a few minutes later. Afterwards Grotowski ex-

181

plains the benefits of this exercise. It is of great importance for actors with a closed or blocked larynx.

During this exercise there was laughter amongst the audience. Grotowski did not hesitate in intervening for silence.

Next Exercise

The pupil lies outstretched on the floor.

Grotowski: "Imagine you are lying in a warm river and the warm water is flowing over your body. Remain in silence for a little while, then sing."

In the meantime, Grotowski touches with his hand the parts of the body that come into contact with the warm water. The pupil must simply react.

In my opinion these exercises serve to stimulate the voice centres which are nearest to the place or person that you are speaking to, or by whom the impulse is given.

Another exercise with the same purpose

Lie on your stomach on the floor.

— The pupil is instructed to talk to the ceiling
— The voice centres to be used are in the back, i. e. below the neck, in the lower part of the back around the midriff and between the shoulder blades

Exercises based on animal sounds

Tiger: A roar, prolonged, and continuing in the same intonation and breath.

Snake: A hiss, prolonged, and continuing in the same intonation and breath.

Cow: A moo, prolonged, and continuing in the same intonation and breath.

During these exercises the body must accentuate the sounds produced. The most elementary movements of each of these animals must be portrayed by the body.

Again with this exercise Grotowski goes a little further. He sets off definite reactions in the pupil by using, for example, an aggressive attitude towards him.

Further exercises with animals as their theme

The actor is a bull and Grotowski the bull-fighter, with a red pull-over that he has found somewhere. The actor must attack while singing.

During this exercise Grotowski interrupts for a moment to give some explanations. The actors have a short pause, but are not allowed to speak together or even whisper.

Grotowski: "All these techniques used with the vocal exercises are the opposite of normal methods. During lessons in diction only consonants are studied. There are special lessons dealing with vowels in which a musical instrument is used, such as a piano. During these lessons much attention is paid to respiration and different breathing techniques. This is wrong. Abdominal respiration, for instance, cannot be mastered by everyone. People adapt their respiration according to their human activities. Their activity conditions their breathing. Be careful only to suggest an improved method of respiration to someone who has genuine difficulties with his breathing. It is foolish to impose a specific type of respiration or a certain technique on a person who has no problems in this respect. This is what happens in most theatre schools however. **The type of respiration a person uses must be tended.**

Furthermore, there is one absolute rule

Bodily activity comes first, and then vocal expression.

Most actors work in the opposite order.

First you bang on the table and afterwards you shout!

The vocal process cannot be free without a well functioning

183

larynx. The larynx must first be relaxed, and then the chin and jaws.

If the larynx does not relax and open, you must try to find a way to make it do so. That is why I asked the third pupil to stand on his head. If he does this, and at the same time speaks, shouts or sings, there is a good chance that the larynx will open. I knew an actress who was suffering from a severe vocal crisis. The doctors couldn't help her. Once, in public, I gave her some hard blows on the cheek. The result was that she began to sing spontaneously.

In this connection a whole process can be mentioned:

Contact – Observation – Stimulus – Reaction

In the vocal process, all the parts of the body must vibrate. It is of the utmost importance – and I shall go on repeating this – that we learn to speak with the body first and then with the voice.

To pick up an object from a table is the conclusion of a complicated process in the body.

Observation – Stimuli – Reactions (answer)

The voice is something material. It can be used for everything. All the body's stimuli can be expressed by the voice. Just think of the association possibilities of the voice in connection with the following words, for example:

- Knife
- Soft
- Snake
- Dog

The body must be a centre of reactions. We must learn to respond to everything with our body, even to an everyday conversation. We must gradually try to banish all physical formality from our behaviour: crossed arms hamper our reactions.

All these things – voice and body expressions – must be learnt individually by each of us. Therefore a regular daily check-up of all that concerns our body and our voice is essential. The teacher or adviser should only intervene when difficulties arise. He should

184

never interrupt the personal process as long as this stands a good chance of achieving results, and certainly not try to change it. The natural physiological process – respiration, voice, movement – must never be restricted or obstructed by wrongly imposed systems and theories."

Some more remarks regarding the voice

"The human voice seeks resounding elements. The body, and especially those parts of it already mentioned, is the first and right place for the resonance of the voice.

'On est créateur seulement quand on fait des recherches.'

This is also the case with the theatre. For each situation and for its interpretation by the voice you can try to find the appropriate resonance. This applies to the training but not to the preparation of the role. Exercises and creative work should never be mingled. Milieu, the spirit of the age, mentality, can all be serious obstacles to the formation of a good voice.

The most elementary fault, and that in most urgent need of correction, is the over-straining of the voice because one forgets to speak with the body.

Voice training in most countries and at nearly all schools is wrongly conceived and practised. The natural voice process is hampered and destroyed. Unnatural techniques are learnt and these spoil the original good habits.

My main principle is: **Do not think of the vocal instrument itself, do not think of the words, but react – react with the body.**

The body is the first vibrator and resonator."

*　　*　　*

Grotowski: "Today we shall demonstrate certain exercises that will seem impossible for you to perform at present. Observe Mr. Cieslak attentively. Only observation can help you to master these exercises in a short time."

Cieslak's exercise consisted mainly of the following:
- Concentration
- Rolling and turning of the body, in an upright position
- Shoulderstands (position standing on the shoulders)
- Outstretched on the floor – rolling and turning of the body
- Leaps: a whole series of these to be performed without a pause, becoming more and more difficult

Note: The pupils are asked to do these same exercises as best they can.

Most of the exercises seem to me to be based on the principle of yoga exercises. More than a coincidental similarity can be observed. Particularly worthy of notice is Cieslak's deep and constant concentration. All his movements have a well-defined direction that is followed by all the extremities and, on closer observation, even by all the muscles. The essential difference between these exercises and yoga is that these are dynamic exercises aimed at the exterior. This exteriorization replaces the introversion typical of yoga.

After the leaps, a compulsory pause for relaxation follows.

These exercises were collective. Now Cieslak starts to work with each pupil individually.

The cat
Cat improvisations. Cieslak gives an example: a cat that stretches and relaxes after having slept.

The main aim of this exercise, as with many of the others, is to make the vertebral column supple.

Grotowski and Cieslak insist on these exercises being done barefoot. It is essential to feel contact with the floor.

Shoulderstand exercises, supported by one bent arm
First an explanation is given on how to fall. This involves a special technique which, if practised correctly, allows a painless fall from any position.

186

After the demonstration, all the pupils are invited to do the same exercise.

From all the efforts it is apparent that the greatest difficulty lies in the discovery of the point where balance is reached and under control. Grotowski intervenes and points out that you must search for this point without haste and without great exertion. Everyone must experience it for himself.

Note: It is obvious from this exercise that our student actors have not had sufficient physical training. Furthermore, it proves that it is necessary to take the physical condition of our actors more seriously and devote more time to it. It is not enough to be able to fall off a ladder without being hurt. That is simply a question of acrobatics and can be done by anyone with daring. The real problem is to acquire a firm technique of movement which allows us to control even the smallest movement in every detail. What an embarrassing sight it is to see an actor go down on his knees with a grimace on his face and creaking joints!

Cieslak demonstrates a whole gamut of movements. Each movement is accompanied by an indescribable concentration and complete control of both body and respiration.

Elbowstand

This is a headstand supported by both elbows instead of the palms of the hands. The hands are joined at the back of the head. This exercise aids the sense of balance.

65–67 Elbowstand.

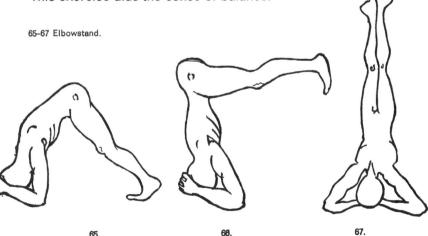

65.   66.   67.

Next exercise

Kneel with the legs slightly apart, the chest arched forward by an impulsion from the loins. Next the body bends slowly backwards until the head touches the ground, the loins pushing continually forward in order to keep the arch and maintain balance. It is also through the pushing forward of the loins that the body lifts itself back to its original position. The chest must remain arched all the time, even in the final position, otherwise the exercise is useless. This is yet another exercise to improve the suppleness of the vertebral column (68).

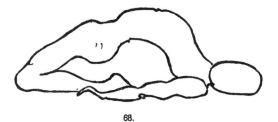

68.

Shoulderstand

Kneel ready to take the position for the headstand. Make a triangle of the forearms, with the palms of the hands on the back of the head. In the final position, it is the shoulders that are the supporting point.

Here again it is of the utmost importance not to hurry. This exercise has the greatest chance of success if one searches unhurriedly for the point of balance.

"Take your time", Grotowski repeats once more.

Slow Motion

- Start from a standing position
- From a headstand, change to a shoulderstand (cf. previous exercise)
- With the legs still in the air, transfer the weight of the body from the shoulder to the back of the neck, the arms and hands on the ground for support

188

– Rolling – still in slow motion – with legs outstreched
– Return to original standing position

This exercise must be done with a certain imaginary force. You must imagine you are in constant contact with someone in order to give the exercise a definite direction.

The great expressive force of this exercise lies in the control of the leg muscles. The toes are constantly stretched in a fixed direction. When one of the legs reaches the point at the end of the movement on the ground, the arm takes over. Here co-ordination is essential. Just before the leg movement finishes, the arm starts moving in the same direction and in the same way.

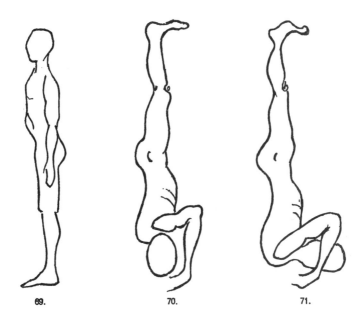

69.   70.   71.

69–75 Slow Motion.

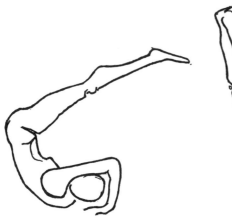

72.

73.

74.

75.

Hand/finger exercise

Cieslak gives an example of a game with the hands. Amazing! This is a game with a butterfly and a bit of fluff. The arm and hand must be well loosened first. While completely relaxed, the hand is made to vibrate by the muscles of the upper arm. Only these muscles are activated at that moment.

During the exercise **one** hand is continuously in full action.

Thus the left hand is the protecting one and the right hand the active, grasping one.

Exercise consisting of the co-ordination of various parts of an arbitrary cycle

The process is as follows:

- To embrace
- To take
- To take for oneself
- To possess
- To protect

All these elements must be linked together in a co-ordinated movement. It is of the greatest importance that the vertebral column be continuously activated throughout this exercise. **The vertebral column is the centre of expression. The driving impulse, however, stems from the loins. Every live impulse begins in this region, even if invisible from the outside.**

Following Cieslak's example, the pupils are made to repeat this process, first individually and then in pairs. In the latter case a certain association already exists:

- To embrace
- To take
- To push away

We have already pointed out Grotowski's all-important principle: first the body and then the voice. Here he emphasizes once again how in this exercise it is essential that the body begin the movement which is then taken up by the hands. The hands are, in a sense, a substitute for the voice. They are used to accentuate the

191

body's objective, the movement's impulse coming from the vertebral column. Thus the exercise must start **in** the body, the vertebral column and the trunk. This process must be visible.

The last part of the exercise is the pushing away.

The pushing away is the result of the whole process and is done by the hands. It must be a concrete movement. The impulse, however, must precede the movement itself. This impulse must visibly come from the body. It originates and develops in the loins. The hands do not come into action before the end of the process. For the actor, the core of the exercise is to be conscious of the fact that an internal pushing away must take place before the actual pushing away. This exercise too must be done slowly, unhurriedly. The direction in this case is given by the position of the chest.

After the exercises Grotowski gives some supplementary explanations:

"In this exercise we have given you some details to help you analyse a movement. I hope it is clear from this that it is very important **never** to do anything that does not harmonize with your vital impulse, something **you yourself cannot account for.**

The earth binds us. When we jump into the air, it awaits us.

Everything we undertake must be done without too much haste, but with great courage; in other words, not like a sleep-walker but in all consciousness, dynamically, as a result of definite impulses. We must gradually learn to be personally responsible for all we do. We must search. All these exercises can be enriched with new elements and personal experiences if we search for them.

This searching must be directed particularly towards the adaptation of the body to the gesture and vice versa. Our body must adapt itself to each movement."

Grotowski insists on all his exercises being executed with a minimum of clothes on. Practically naked. Nothing must hinder our movements. Above all, no shoes of any kind for these prevent the feet from **living,** from **moving.** Our feet must touch the floor. This contact must make them live.

Once more Grotowski returns to his golden rule: "Our whole body must adapt to every movement, however small. Everybody must proceed in his own way. No stereotype exercises can be imposed. If we pick up a piece of ice from the ground, our whole body must react to this movement and to the cold. Not only the fingertips, not only the whole hand, but the whole body must reveal the coldness of this little piece of ice."

Another series of exercises follows. These are executed by Cieslak, and they show how the body has to adapt to each movement. All the exercises that were practised in detail and separately during the former lessons, are now executed by Cieslak in one co-ordinated movement. He links them up in one complete cycle. His entire body adapts itself to each movement, to the slightest detail. With unbroken concentration and control of all his muscles – and there are many – he works through the whole cycle, improvising around it. This lasts for about fifteen minutes.

When you master these exercises so that you can execute this cycle without too much technical hindrance, you can begin to combine them with an improvisation. The exercises are then only pretexts or, in Grotowski's words "details". While performing the exercise Cieslak linked all these details into an improvisation without any preparation. **No preparation is allowed.**

Only authenticity is necessary, absolutely obligatory. The improvisation must be completely unprepared, otherwise all naturalness will be destroyed. What's more, the whole improvisation has no sense if the details are not executed with precision.

Connection between the exercises and the performance

The exercises only serve as a spring-board for the situations and the details of the play. On stage you have to be individual. The exercises adapted to the situations of the play must have a perso-

193

nal cachet, and the co-ordination of the various elements must also be individual.

That which comes from the inside is half improvised. That which is outward is technique.

In all the exercises composing the cycle executed by Grotowski's companion, Cieslak, there is never a sign of symmetry.

If something is symmetrical it is not organic!

Symmetry is a concept of gymnastics, not of physical education for the theatre. The theatre requires organic movements.

The significance of a movement depends on the personal interpretation. To the spectator, the movements of the actor on the stage can have quite a different meaning from that of the actor himself.

It is wrong to think that the exercises which Mr. Cieslak shows us – physical exercises – are only for athletes, for people with strong, lithe bodies.

Everybody can create his own series of movements, a store that he can draw on if the intimate experience demands it. However, he must not forget to eliminate all that lies outside it. This store should not only contain movements but preferably also the composing elements of these movements.

* * *

After one of the lessons Grotowski gave instructions to prepare an improvisation exercise, based on the various details and exercises that were demonstrated and taught by Cieslak during the same lesson.

At the beginning of the third lesson the pupils are divided into two groups. They are separately asked to show their improvisation.

Immediately one is struck by the great lack of continuity amongst the pupils. The essence of this improvisation exercise is simply to achieve unbroken continuity between the different parts of the exercise.

When both groups have demonstrated the exercises, Grotowski

makes some remarks on execution and technical finish. The main faults are lack of continuity, as already mentioned, and loss of balance in the various positions. This is mainly due to hastiness.

Every pupil must overcome his own difficulties. Grotowski and Cieslak correct each pupil, after which he has to repeat the difficult part of the exercise until it is perfect.

When making a correction you must always search for the origin of the fault and not concentrate too much on the fault itself.

Cieslak demonstrates the exercise once more, stopping whenever he comes to difficulties that have bothered most of the pupils. It becomes clear that the principal reasons for such difficulties are lack of control and too much haste.

The way in which Grotowski always involves the pupil himself in the discovery of faults and unnecessary movements is remarkable. Together they try to perfect the exercises. Thus Cieslak draws attention to a girl who, as she meets the floor in a somersault, obviously does not know **why** she is doing it. This is an error. **No association was present.** She repeats the exercise and Cieslak finds out that the fault is due to a technical obstacle. A certain gesture was prepared in advance and blocked the whole continuity of the exercise. Prepared gestures must be avoided. Only at the moment the gesture is made must it link up with a spontaneous association.

A fault that is due to the weakness of the abdominal muscles can be eliminated by a slight alteration: for example, by the unnoticed support of the hands. This is only done to improve the technical performance. Technical faults do not interfere with the association which comes at a later stage. Cieslak illustrates this with an example.

Even while lying stretched out on the floor as part of an exercise, you must be conscious all the time of having a reason for doing this. You must associate it with something.

When co-ordinating the parts of the exercise, you must constantly seek for the best method of co-ordination without trying to find new associations at that moment. Only through perfect control of the different exercises can you perform the whole cycle around

195

an association you have already found. The score of the separate exercises is not fixed. Everyone must experiment for himself in order to find out the right positions and methods of execution. This is the essential basis for the education of actors.

Relaxation of the tired vertebral column
The ideal position for relaxation is to squat with the head almost touching the ground in front of you, the arms stretched out in front and the palms resting on the floor (76).

76.

Hand and finger exercises
Most actors and actresses have stiff hands and fingers. These extremities have a great power of expression. Therefore they must be kept lithe and supple. There are many important hand and finger exercises for this purpose. Cieslak demonstrates a whole series of these.

*   *   *

Grotowski begins with vocal exercises. These are specially intended for those pupils who did not have a chance to participate previously.
The four pupils who went through the whole cycle at the beginning start with this once again, this time without interruption:

196

- Stimulation of the voice
- Obtaining an echo: conversation with the wall, the ceiling, the floor, etc.

Here Grotowski gives some explanation: "If you expect an answer from the wall in the form of an echo, your whole body must react to this possible answer. If you give me an answer, you must first do so with your body. It is alive. Now try to do the same with the wall. The exercises which use the echo help to exteriorize the voice. The actor must react towards the exterior, attacking the space around him, in contact all the time with another person or persons. He must never listen to himself as this results in the introversion of the voice. Often, however, the actor is unable to resist the temptation to listen to himself, in which case he must listen to the **echo** of his voice."

Grotowski now concentrates on two pupils
To determine their voice type he starts the two pupils off with a conversation game. The game begins with the thorough mutual observation of both partners, whereby they must find out with which parts of the body they will talk to each other.
Next Grotowski gives an exercise that prepares all the parts of the body for contact with the partner, or rather activates them.
This exercise activates the following parts of the body:
- Feet
- Knees
- Thighs
- Lower abdomen – abdomen
- Chest
- Arms and hands
The body converses.
After these preparatory exercises the voice joins in.

197

Grotowski now begins to work with one pupil at a time
He stimulates, by short strokes with the joined fingertips, the pupil's centres of energy that are spread all over the body.
In this connection the main places are:
– Between the shoulder blades
– The lower part of the back
– The head: top and occiput
– The chest: at the sides where the ribs are attached
The actor must be able to arouse these stimuli and activate them by repeated exercise. This must be done by the voice and from the inside. It is totally wrong to use the method of striking oneself. To reach the different places you must let the body undergo certain transformations. To speak when the body is twisted in an unnatural position can never be right. Such unnatural positions may be used only when they are intentional, in which case they are quite harmless to the voice. In fact, they can be beneficial as for example with the exercise for the opening of the larynx. The pupil stands on his head and must talk, sing and shout for some time in this position.

Vocal exercises
– Exercise to stimulate the voice centres
– Exercise for the voice based on the HEE-sound:
  From very low to very high
  From very soft to very loud
  From very long to very short
– The same exercise but now with the HA-sound
– After this comes the tiger interpretation that is referred to earlier
In these exercises it is particularly important never to make any pauses. It would seem to be of great importance for the pupils to use texts they know perfectly by heart during the vocal exercises. If they have to think about improvising a text, then the continuity is broken. Knowing a few songs by heart would also appear to be very useful.
During these different exercises you must free yourself totally of

198

the text. Searching for the text involves a thinking process, and that is exactly what has to be avoided.

After the vocal exercises Grotowski lets every pupil do a relaxation exercise. This consists in resting for about 20 minutes, during which time neither speaking nor whispering is allowed. Cold drinks can also have a bad effect on the voice.

Next Grotowski answers some questions from the audience:

1) "Why is one not allowed to talk or whisper after these exercises?"

    Grotowski: "To most of the pupils these exercises are quite new. The voice instrument has not yet become adapted to these techniques. It has produced sounds that it has never produced before. Silence is the best way of protecting the voice instrument that has been slightly influenced by these exercises."

2) "Does the text play a part in these exercises? Can it be just any text?"

    Grotowski: "I don't think the text is of great importance. By this I mean that it can be fortuitous, even that it must be fortuitous. The important thing is to give this text, through the body and the vocal technique, a degree of interest that it does not have under normal circumstances. By means of these exercises, movements and vocal techniques, you try to draw attention. During the performance this means the attention of the audience."

Exercises to activate the body's different resonators

Somebody from the audience is asked to come and touch the different resonators in order to convince himself that the part of the body in question does actually vibrate if they are used correctly. If the actor masters all the vocal techniques, he can attain a resonance in the most improbable parts of the body.

For an immediate contact with the public and for delivering a

speech, it is very important to be able to activate the main resonators.

Association exercises
The pupil has to sing a song while conjuring up an association
with the following:
- A tiger
- A snake
- A wriggling snake
- A knife – to cut
- An axe – to hew

Then he has to "sing" a sheet of paper out of Grotowski's hand
from a yard's distance.
Next he has to sing a song during which the voice must make
contact with a particular spot on the ceiling. The voice is like an
arm which must try to reach the indicated spot.

After these association exercises Grotowski proves the existence of the vibrations in the different resonators
Grotowski asks the pupil to place the resonance in the back of
the head (occiput). He strikes a match and holds it a short
distance from the resonant spot. The flame does indeed move,
vibrate.
In the same way Grotowski has made a glass break during an
exercise with his actors simply through vibration.
Thus he also proves that the voice is a material force.
It is evident that for these exercises Grotowski's techniques must
be mastered perfectly.
The advanced stage of his scientific research involving voice
and movement is proved by these effects. In this respect it is
worth noting that Grotowski himself always lays stress upon
discipline as the indispensable keystone to all that leads to a
result.

Questions

1) "Is it possible to stimulate yourself from the outside? In other words, is it possible to stimulate your own voice centres by hitting or pinching yourself?"

Grotowski: "This is impossible, even dangerous! You hereby lose your natural attitude. In trying to reach these different places, our body is automatically placed in an unnatural position and consequently the vocal organs cannot execute their function normally.

From my experience of this method, I think I may also go so far as to point out the psychological repercussions resulting from this mistaken practice. If you begin to stimulate and activate your own voice centres there is a risk that, because of a sporadic result, you may begin to think this method effective, in spite of all the dangers it involves for the voice and the organs that produce and form the voice. In this respect I think I may even speak of a certain narcissism."

2) "You have given us a number of technical details, but what about your philosophy of art?"

Grotowski: "A philosophy always comes **after** a technique! Tell me: do you walk home with your legs or your ideas?

There are many actors who, during rehearsals, like to enter into scientific and stilted discussions about art and so on. These actors try through these discussions to hide their lack of engagement and their lack of a maximum exertion. If you give yourself completely during a rehearsal you do not want to discuss. In discussion you hide yourself behind a false mask."

After this interruption Grotowski continues with the lesson.

In the following exercises the emphasis will be laid upon associations and the adaptation of the voice to these associations.

Grotowski points out that all symmetry of movement must be avoided. Actors are educated for the theatre and not for gymnastics.

Associations
1) Think of a cow in a meadow. Take the position of this cow. Stomach downwards. Adapt your voice. Talk to the ground as a cow would. Place the voice in the abdomen, but wait for an answer, an echo, from the floor.
2) Think of a singing tiger. Sing a song and roar the notes, without forgetting the melody. In spite of these associations, pay attention to the fact that the body must act first. The body must, by seeking for the position and the direction, facilitate the task of the voice.

Mask
Grotowski: "Sing your name ... Joseph. Sing Joseph. Evoke this Joseph. Who is he, this stranger? Go on singing your name – Joseph – asking: Joseph, who are you? What are you? Find the mask of Joseph's face. Is this really Joseph's mask? Yes, this is the essential Joseph. And now it is this essential Joseph, his mask, that sings."

We notice that the pupil's voice changes, deepens, and becomes unrecognizable.

*　　*　　*

After a short pause all the pupils are invited to come forward. Grotowski asks them to think of an animal which each must choose bearing in mind his preference or his affection for that particular animal. After a short period of concentration he must try to express the sounds the chosen animal can make, but this process must first pass through the whole body. In other words, the body must adapt itself organically to the impulses that precede the sound. So it is necessary first to express the animal with the body.

Analysis of the exercise
1) Gradually start to seek for the chosen animal with the body – do not hurry.
2) If you think you have found the animal's right impulses, then

202

begin to activate the voice. Start to give the animal voice through a text, or a song.

3) Enact the lovemaking of two animals. Use the voice.

Here the body is all the more the principal factor.

The second part of the exercise starts with the voice. This means that one must first catch and work out the impulses for some time until they are so strong that you **must** give voice to them.

In the next exercise, each pupil has to compare himself to a plant or a tree. This process inevitably starts on the ground. How does a plant grow?

– The plant talks
– The plant sings
– The silence of a plant

The silence of a tree . . . This silence can be heard, says Grotowski. The wind in the trees – the wind becomes stronger – becomes a storm – the whole wood moves.

Suddenly he interrupts the different interpretations and passes on to another aspect.

– The tree sings in the sun
– In the tree birds are singing

All these different interpretations take place with movement and text!

Grotowski points out the danger that lurks behind this kind of exercise

"In these exercises, it is easy to cheat and avoid the natural impulses, simply imitating from outside the form of the plant. You can, of course, begin by composition, but this is a different exercise. Thinking is not allowed in these exercises either. You must immediately work out the first impulse within yourself, even if the result differs widely from that of your colleagues. Never look at the others, and above all do not copy their results. **The people around you don't exist.** What you are doing belongs to your intimate self and concerns nobody else."

203

Finally Grotowski gives a short survey of the most important elements and rules of his technique:
- "Imprint on your memory: the **body** must work first. Afterwards comes the **voice.**
- If you start on something, you must be fully engaged in it. You must give yourself one hundred per cent, your whole body, your whole mind and all its possible, individual, most intimate associations. During a rehearsal an actor may reach a climax that he will work on. He keeps the same gestures and the same positions but never again reaches the same intimate climax. **The peak of a climax can never be rehearsed. You must only exercise the preparatory stages of the process that leads to the heights of that climax. A climax cannot be reached without practice. The climax itself can never be reproduced.**
- In all you do you must keep in mind that there are no fixed rules, no stereotypes. The essential thing is that everything must come from and through the body. First and foremost, there must be a physical reaction to everything that affects us. Before reacting with the voice, you must first react with the body. If you think, you must think with your body. However, it is better not to think but to act, to take risks. When I tell you not to think, I mean with the head. Of course you must think, but with the body, logically, with precision and responsibility. You must think with the whole body, by means of actions. Don't think of **the result,** and certainly not of how beautiful the result may be. If it grows spontaneously and organically, like live impulses, finally mastered, it will always be beautiful – far more beautiful than any amount of calculated results put together.
My terminology has arisen from personal experience and personal research. Everybody must find an expression, a wording of his own, a strictly personal way to condition his own feelings."

The Actor's Technique

In 1967 Jerzy Grotowski's Theatre Laboratory performed **The Constant Prince** at the **Théâtre des Nations** in Paris. After a tour of Denmark, Sweden and Norway in 1966, this trip to Paris gave to a greater audience the chance of judging for itself the results achieved by his method. It was during his stay in Paris that Jerzy Grotowski recorded this interview with Denis Bablet which was then printed in **Les Lettres Françaises** (Paris, 16/22 March 1967). Translation: Amanda Pasquier and Judy Barba.

Jerzy Grotowski, I would first like you to define for me your position with regard to various acting theories as, for example, those of Stanislavski, Artaud and Brecht, explaining how, through reflection and due naturally to your personal experience, you have come to elaborate your own technique for the actor, defining both its aims and means.

I think it is necessary to distinguish between **methods** and **aesthetics**. Brecht, for example, explained many very interesting things about the possibilities of a way of acting which involved the actor's discursive control over his actions, the Verfremdungs-effekt. But this was not really a method. It was rather a kind of aesthetic duty demanded of the actor, for Brecht did not actually ask himself: "How can this be done?". Although he has provided certain explanations, these are only general ... Certainly Brecht did study the technique of the actor in great detail, but always from the standpoint of the producer observing the actor.

Artaud's case is different. Artaud presents an indisputable stimulus where research relative to the possibilities of the actor is concerned, but what he proposes are in the end only visions, a

205

sort of poem about the actor, and no practical conclusions can be drawn from his explanations. Artaud was well aware – as we know from his essay **Un Athlétisme Affectif** in **Le Théâtre et son Double** – that there is an authentic parallelism between the efforts of a man who works with his body (e.g. picking up a heavy object) and the psychic processes (e.g. receiving a blow, retalliating). He knew that the body possesses a centre that decides the reactions of the athlete, and those of the actor who wants to reproduce psychic efforts through his body. But if one analyses his principles from a practical point of view, one discovers that they lead to stereotypes: a particular type of movement to exteriorize a particular type of emotion. In the end this leads to clichés.

But there was no cliché when Artaud was doing his research and, as an actor, observed his own reactions, seeking an escape from the exact imitation of human reactions and calculated reconstructions. But let us consider his theory. It certainly contains a useful stimulus. However, if one treats it as a technique, one ends in clichés. Artaud represents a fruitful starting point for research and an aesthetic point of view. When he asks the actor to study his breathing, to exploit the different elements of respiration in his acting, he is offering him the chance of widening his possibilities, of acting not only through words but also through that which is inarticulate (inspiration, expiration, etc.). This is a very fertile aesthetic proposition. It is not a technique.

There are, in fact, very few acting **methods.** The most developed is that of Stanislavski. Stanislavski propounded the most important questions and he supplied his own answers. Throughout his numerous years of research his method evolved, but his disciples did not. Stanislavski had disciples for each of his periods, and each disciple stuck to his particular period; hence the discussions of a theological order. Stanislavski was always experimenting himself and he did not suggest recipes, but the means whereby the actor might discover himself, replying in all concrete situations to the question: "How can this be done?". This is essential. He naturally brought all this about within the setting of the theatre of his country, his time, of a realism which . . .

. . . An interior realism . . .

. . . An existential realism, I think, or rather an existential naturalism. Charles Dullin also devised many good exercises, improvisations, games with masks, or again exercises with such themes as "man and plants", "man and animals". These are very useful for the preparation of the actor. They stimulate not only his imagination, but also the development of his natural reactions. This, however, does not constitute a technique for the formation of the actor.

What then is the originality of your position in relation to these diverse conceptions?

All conscious systems in the field of acting ask the question: "How can this be done?". This is as it should be. A method is the consciousness of this "how". I believe that one must ask oneself this question once in one's life, but as soon one enters into the details it must no longer be asked for, at the very moment of formulating it, one begins to create stereotypes and clichés. One must then ask the question: "What must I **not** do?".

Technical examples are always the clearest. Let us take respiration. If we ask the question: "How should I breathe?", we will work out a precise, perfect type of breathing, perhaps the abdominal type. It is indeed a fact that children, animals, people who are closest to nature, breathe principally with the abdomen, the diaphragm. But then we come to the second question: "What sort of abdominal respiration is the best?". And we could try to

207

discover among numerous examples a type of inspiration, a type of expiration, a particular position for the vertebral column. This would be a terrible mistake for there is no perfect type of respiration valid for everyone, nor for all psychical and physical situations. Breathing is a physiological reaction linked with specific characteristics in each of us and which is dependent on situations, types of effort, physical activities. It is the natural thing for most people, when breathing freely, to use abdominal respiration. The number of types of abdominal respiration, however, are unlimited. And of course there are exceptions. For example, I have met actresses who, because their thoraxes were too long, could not naturally use abdominal breathing in their work. For them it was therefore necessary to find another type of breathing controlled by the vertebral column. If the actor tries artificially to impose on himself the perfect, objective abdominal respiration, he blocks the natural process of respiration, even if his is naturally of the diaphragmatic type.

When I begin to work with an actor, the first question I ask myself is: "Does this actor have any breathing difficulties?". He breathes well; he has enough air to speak, to sing. Why then create a problem by imposing on him a different type of respiration? This would be absurd. On the other hand, perhaps he does have difficulties. Why? Are there physical problems? ... Psychical problems? If he has psychical problems, what kind of problems are they?

For example, an actor is contracted. Why is he contracted? We are all contracted in one way or another. One cannot be completely relaxed as is taught in many theatre schools, for he who is totally relaxed is nothing more than a wet rag. Living is not being contracted, nor is it being relaxed: it is a process. But if the actor is always too contracted, the cause blocking the natural respiratory process – almost always of a psychical or psychological nature – must be discovered. We must determine which is his natural type of respiration. I observe the actor, while suggesting exercises that compel him into total psycho-physical mobilisation. I watch him while in a moment of conflict, play or flirtation with another actor, in those moments when something changes automatically. Once we know the actor's natural type of respiration, we can more exactly define the factors which act as obstacles to his natural reactions and the aim of the exercises is then to eliminate them. Here lies the essential difference between our technique and the other methods: ours is a negative technique, not a positive one.

We are not after the recipes, the stereotypes which are the prerogative of professionals. We do not attempt to answer questions such as: "How does one show irritation? How should one walk? How should Shakespeare be played?". For these are the sort of questions usually asked. Instead, one must ask the actor: "What are the obstacles blocking you on your way towards the total act which must engage all your psycho-physical resources, from the most instinctive to the most rational?". We must find out what it is that hinders him in the way of respiration, movement and – most important of all – human contact. What resistances are there? How can they be eliminated? I want to take away, steal from the actor all that disturbs him. That which is creative will remain within him. It is a liberation. If nothing remains, it means he is not creative.

One of the greatest dangers threatening the actor is, of course, lack of discipline, chaos. One cannot express oneself through anarchy. I believe there can be no true creative process within the actor if he lacks discipline or spontaneity. Meyerhold based his work on discipline, exterior formation; Stanislavski on the spontaneity of daily life. These are, in fact, the two complementary aspects of the creative process.

But what do you mean by the actor's "total act"?

209

It is not only the mobilisation of all the resources of which I have spoken. It is also something far more difficult to define, although very tangible from the point of view of work. It is the act of laying oneself bare, of tearing off the mask of daily life, of exteriorizing oneself. Not in order to "show oneself off", for that would be exhibitionism. It is a serious and solemn act of revelation. The actor must be prepared to be absolutely sincere. It is like a step towards the summit of the actor's organism in which consciousness and instinct are united.

In practice, then, the formation of the actor must be adapted to each case.

Yes, I don't believe in recipes.

Therefore there is no such thing as the formation of actors, but the formation of each individual actor. How do you go about this? You observe them? You question them? And then? ...

There are exercises. We speak very little. During the training each actor is asked to search for his own associations, his personal variants (recalling memories, evoking his needs, all that he has not been able to fulfil).

Do you train collectively?

The starting point of the training is the same for everyone. However, let us take as an example the physical exercises. The elements of the exercises are the same for all, but everyone must perform them in terms of his own personality. An onlooker can easily see the differences according to the individual personalities.

210

The essential problem is to give the actor the possibility of working "in security". The work of the actor is in danger; it is submitted to continuous supervision and observation. An atmosphere must be created, a working system in which the actor feels that he can do absolutely anything, will be understood and accepted. It is often at the moment when the actor understands this that he reveals himself.

There is therefore total confidence between the different actors, and between them and you.

There is no question of the actor having to do what the producer proposes. He must realize that he can do whatever he likes and that even if in the end his own suggestions are not accepted, they will never be used against him.

He will be judged and not condemned ...

He must be accepted as a human being, as he is.

Regarding the actor's integration into the performance, you readily use the term "score" and not "role". This nuance is obviously very important in your work. Could you define exactly what you mean by the actor's "score"?

What is the role? In fact it is almost always a character's text, the typed text that is given to the actor. It is also a particular conception of the character, and here again there is a stereotype. Hamlet is an intellectual without greatness, or else a revolutionary who wants to change everything. The actor has his text; next an encounter is necessary. It must not be said that the role is a pretext for the actor, nor the actor a pretext for the role. It is an instrument for making a cross-section of oneself, analysing oneself and thereby re-establishing contact with others. If he is content with explaining the role, the actor will know that he has to sit down here, cry out there. At the beginning of rehearsals, associations will be evoked normally, but after twenty performances there will be nothing left. The acting will be purely mechanical.

To avoid this the actor, like the musician, needs a score. The musician's score consists of notes. Theatre is an encounter. The actor's score consists of the elements of human contact: "give and take". Take other people, confront them with oneself, one's own experiences and thoughts, and give a reply. In these somewhat intimate human encounters there is always this element of "give and take". The process is repeated, but always **hic et nunc:** that is to say it is never quite the same.

For each production this score is gradually established between the actor and you?

Yes, in a sort of collaboration.

So the actor is free. How does he manage (and this was one of the great problems underlined by Stanislavski) to find for each performance the creative state which allows him to execute the score without it becoming too rigid, without a purely mechanical discipline setting in? How can the vital existence of the score and creative liberty of the actor both be preserved?

It is difficult to reply in a few words, but if you will allow me a popularization I shall answer: if during rehearsals the actor has

212

established the score as something natural, organic (the pattern of his reactions, "give and take"), and if, before performing, he is prepared to make this confession, hiding nothing, then each performance will attain its plenitude.

"Give and take" ... Does this include the spectator too?

One must not think of the spectator while acting. Naturally this is a delicate question. Firstly the actor structures his role; secondly, the score. At that moment he is seeking a sort of purity (the elimination of the superfluous) as well as the signs necessary to expression. Then he thinks: "Is what I am doing comprehensible?". This question implies the presence of the spectator. I myself am there, guiding the work, and I say to the actor: "I don't understand", "I understand" or "I understand but I don't believe" ... Psychologists readily ask the question: "What is your religion?" – not your dogmas or philosophy, but your point of orientation. If the actor has the spectator as his point of orientation, then he will, in a sense, be offering himself for sale.

This will be exhibitionism ...

A sort of prostitution, bad taste ... It is inevitable. A great Polish actor from before the war called it "publicotropism". Yet I don't believe the actor should neglect the fact that the spectator is present and say to himself: "There is no one there", for that would be a lie. In short, the actor must not have the audience as a point of orientation, but at the same time he must not neglect the fact of its presence. You know that in each of our productions we create a different relationship between actors and audience. In **Dr Faustus,** the spectators are the guests; in **The Constant Prince,** they are the onlookers. But I think the essential thing is that the actor must not act **for** the audience, he must act in confrontation with the spectators, in their presence. Better still, he must fulfil an authentic act in place of the spectators, an act of extreme yet disciplined sincerity and authenticity. He must give himself and not hold himself back, open up and not close in on himself as this would end in narcissism.

Do you believe that the actor needs a long preparation before each performance in order to attain what some people call "a state of grace"?

The actor must have time to cast off all the problems and distractions of daily life. In our theatre we have a period of silence lasting thirty minutes during which the actor prepares his costumes, perhaps goes over certain scenes. This is quite natural. A pilot about to try out a new plane for the first time also seeks solitude for a few minutes before taking off.

Do you think that your acting technique is applicable by other producers apart from yourself, that it can be adapted to ends other than yours?

There again one must distinguish between the aesthetic and the method in my work. Of course in the Theatre Laboratory there are the elements of an aesthetic which is personal to me and which must not be copied by others, for the result would be neither authentic nor natural. But we are an institute for research into the art of the actor. Thanks to this technique, the actor can speak and sing in a very wide register. That is an objective result. The fact that when speaking he has no problems with his breathing is also objective. The fact that he can utilise different types of physical and vocal reactions which are very difficult for many people, that again is objective.

214

At present there are, then, two aspects in your work: on the one hand the conscious aesthetic of a creator, and on the other the search for a technique in acting. Which comes first?

The most important thing for me today is to rediscover the elements of the actor's art. I was first trained as an actor, then as a producer. In my early productions in Cracow and Poznan I rejected concessions and theatrical conservatism. Gradually I developed and discovered that to fulfil myself was far less fruitful than studying the possibility of helping others to fulfil themselves. This is not a form of altruism. On the contrary, it is an even greater adventure.

In the end the adventures of a producer become easy, but encounters with other human beings are more difficult, more fruitful and more stimulating. If I can attain from the actor – in collaboration with him – a total self-revelation, as with Ryszard Cieslak in **The Constant Prince,** then this is far more fertile for me than just devising a production or, in other words, creating purely in my own name. I have therefore orientated myself, little by little, towards a para-scientific research in the field of the actor's art. This is the result of a personal evolution and not an initial plan.

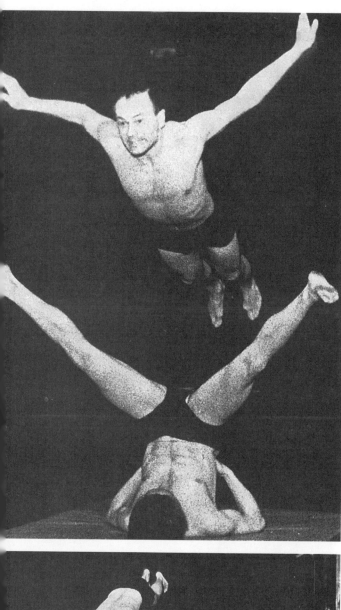

TRAINING

77 - 92 $\longrightarrow$

Photo:
Teatr-Laboratorium
Fredi Graedl

77.

78. | 79.

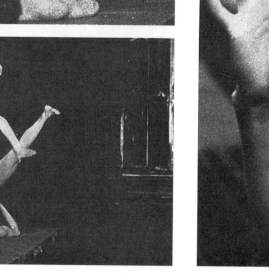

81.

83.

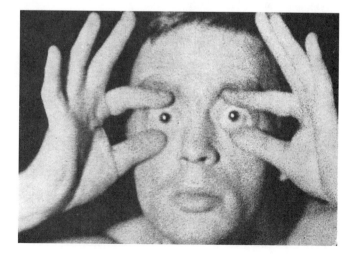

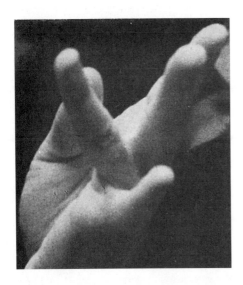

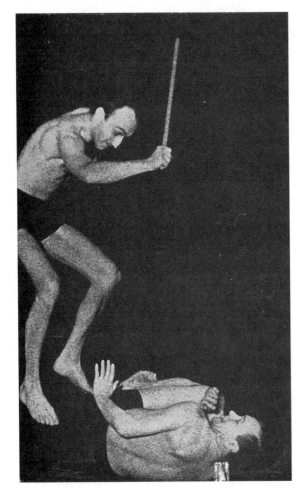

84. 85.

86.

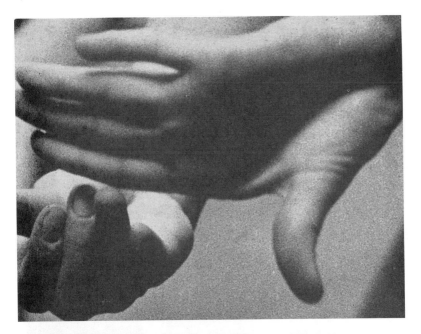

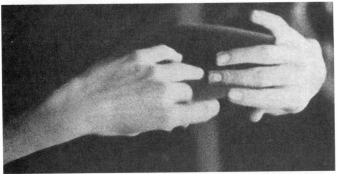

87.

88.

89.   90.

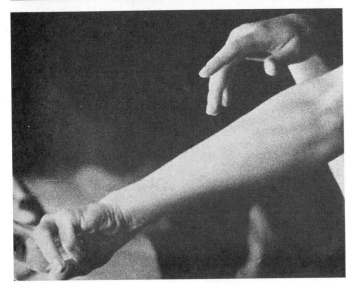

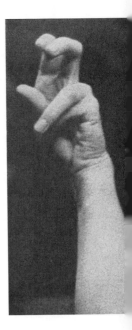

Skara Speech

The following is the text of the closing speech made by Jerzy Grotowski at a 10-day seminar held at the Skara Drama School (Sweden) in January 1966 and directed by him together with his collaborators Ryszard Cieslak, Rena Mirecka and Antoni Jaholkowski. The physical, plastic and vocal exercises referred to are those described in the previous chapters. Translation: Colette Holt.

One cannot teach ready-made methods. You should not try to find out how to play a particular role, how to pitch your voice, how to speak or walk. These are merely clichés and therefore you do not need to bother with them. Do not seek methods ready-made for each occasion because this will only lead to stereotypes. Learn for yourselves your own personal limitations, your own obstacles and how to get round them. After that, whatever you do, do it whole-heartedly. Eliminate from every type of exercise any movement which is purely gymnastic. If you want to do that sort of thing – gymnastics and even acrobatics – always do it as a spontaneous action related to the exterior world, to other people or to objects. Something stimulates you and you react: that is the whole secret. Stimulations, impulses and reactions.

I have spoken much about personal associations, but these associations are not thoughts. They cannot be calculated. Now I make a movement with my hand, then I look for associations. What associations? Perhaps the association that I am touching someone, but this is merely a thought. What is an association in our profession? It is something that springs not only from the mind but also from the body. It is a return towards a precise memory. Do not analyse this intellectually. Memories are always physical

225

reactions. It is our skin which has not forgotten, our eyes which have not forgotten. What we have heard can still resound within us. It is to perform a concrete act, not a movement such as caressing in general but, for example, stroking a cat. Not an abstract cat but a cat which I have seen, with which I have contact. A cat with a specific name – Napoleon, if you like. And it is this particular cat you now caress. These are associations.

Make your actions concrete, relating them to a memory. If you are confident that you are doing this, then do not analyse completely what memory is there – you do it concretely and that is enough. In such a situation, do not dwell on these problems. Speaking of the problems of impulses and reactions, I have underlined throughout this conference that there are no impulses or reactions without contact. A few minutes ago we talked of the problems of contact with an imaginary partner. But this imaginary partner must also be fixed in the space of this actual room. If you do not fix your partner in a precise place your reactions will remain within yourself. That is to say you control yourself, your mind dominates you and you move towards a sort of emotional narcissism, or towards a tension, a kind of restraint.

Contact is one of the most essential things. Often when an actor speaks of contact, or thinks of contact, he believes that it means to gaze fixedly. But this is not contact. It is only a position, a situation. Contact is not staring, it is to see. Now I am in contact with you, I see which of you is against me. I see one person who is indifferent, another who listens with some interest and someone who smiles. All this changes my actions; it is contact, and it forces me to change my way of acting. The pattern is always fixed. In this case, for instance, it is to give you my final advice. I have here some essential notes on what to say, but how I speak depends on contact. If, for example, I hear someone whispering, I speak more loudly and sternly and this unconsciously because of the contact.

226

Thus during the performance where the score – clearly defined text and action – is already fixed, you should always have contact with your partners. Your partner, if he is a good actor, always follows the same score of actions. Nothing is left to chance, no details are changed. But there are minute changes within this set score such that each time he plays in a slightly different way, and you should watch him closely, listen and observe him, responding to his immediate actions. Every day he says "Good morning" with the same intonation, just like your neighbour at home who always says "Good morning" to you. One day he is in a good mood, another day he is tired, another he is in a hurry. He always says "Good morning" but with a slight difference every time. This you must see, not with the mind, but just see and hear. In reality you always give the same response – "Good morning" – but if you have really listened it will be a little different each day. The action and the intonation are the same but the contact is so minute that it is impossible to analyse it rationally. This changes all relationships, and it is also the secret of harmony between men. When a man says "Good morning" and another replies, there is automatically a vocal harmony between the two of them. On the stage we often detect a lack of harmony because the actors don't listen to their partners. The problem is not to listen and ask oneself what the intonation is, only to listen and answer.

I must now speak with an inflection which is unconsciously in harmony with that of my interpreter. It is a concert for two voices and there is immediately a sort of composition since the necessary contact exists. To achieve this there are various exercises. For example, when the play is ready, one day one of the actors may be given the task of playing in an entirely different manner while the others must stick to their fixed score of actions and within this react each in his own way. Here is another exercise: two partners must keep to their set scores, but the motivation behind the action is different. For instance, take a discussion between two friends. On a particular day one friend acts as usual but he is not sincere. There are such slight changes that they are hardly

227

noticeable, but if the partner listens carefully without altering his score he will be able to react accordingly. By means of such exercises contact can be taught. What is the danger of these exercises? The danger is that the actor may change his set score. That is to say he alters his score through changes in situations and actions. That is false. It is easy. You should retain the score and renew the contact every day.

Early roles can be based consciously on vocal resonators but future roles must go beyond this.

Our whole body is a system of resonators – i. e. vibrators – and all these exercises are merely training to widen the possibilities of the voice. The complexity of this system is astonishing. We speak on an impulse, in contact with something or someone. The various positions of the hand change the resonance of the voice. Movements of the spinal column also change the resonance. It is impossible to control all this with the brain. All these exercises with resonators are only a beginning to open the possibilities of the voice and afterwards, when you have already mastered these possibilities, you must live and act without calculated thought. You must progress beyond this and find resonators without any effort. Do not shout during the exercises. You can begin – and this method is all right for many people – with what can be called artificial voices. But as a development of these exercises you should seek another voice, your natural one, and through different impulses of your body, open this voice. Not everyone uses their real voice. Speak naturally and through these natural vocal actions set in motion the various possibilities of the body's resonators. Then there will come a day when your body will know how to resound without prompting. It is the turning point, like the birth of another voice, and can be achieved only by completely natural vocal actions.

How should you work with your voice?

93. **Forefathers' Eve.** The actors evoke ghosts among the spectators during a rural ritual. **Photo: Mozer.**

94. **Forefathers' Eve.** The ghost of a young girl **(Rena Mirecka)** makes contact with the living (the spectators). **Photo: Mozer.**

You should not consciously control yourself. Do not control your body's places of vibration. You should only – and this is the best basic exercise – speak with the various parts of the body. For example, the mouth is on the top of the head and I speak to the ceiling. But I must actually do so; that is I must improvise the text and say: "Mr. Ceiling can you hear me? . . . No? . . . But why won't you listen to me?" Listen whether he speaks, whether he answers. Never listen to your own voice – this is always wrong. It is a physiological rule. If you listen to yourself you block the larynx and block the processes of resonance. Always act, speak, discuss and make contact with concrete things. If you have the impression that your mouth is in your chest, and if you address the wall, you will hear the answer coming from the wall. This is the way to set in motion the whole system of resonances within the body. You can play the part of animals, but the exercises should be developed so that you avoid playing unreal animals, or animals which are remote from your own character. In other words, do not play a dog like a real dog because you are not a dog. Try to find your own dog-like traits. Now I am reacting: I keep my natural voice, and I begin to use my teeth without imitating the voice of a dog. It is a small difference. You can begin by imitating the voice of a dog to explore the possibilities of your vocal imagination but later on in the development you must find your own natural self. Contact is equally important in the physical exercises. The contact which we have seen, with the ground, with the floor, during the exercises is always an authentic dialogue: "Be good to me earth, love me, I have confidence in you. Can you hear me?" And our hands search for this authentic contact.

Then there is the question of dialogue between the different parts of the body. When a hand touches a knee or when a foot touches another foot, all that is a search for security. It is as if the foot was saying: "It is a little painful, but have patience". This is the essence of the dialogue when one foot touches another. This dialogue must always be concrete but not come from the brain. Do not calculate the words of this dialogue. If we do this in an authentic fashion we have the feeling that it is true – now I'm touching my thigh and I'm not thinking of what my dialogue is, but it is a concrete touch.

I have spoken through my hand to my thigh. Everyone must search in his own fashion. If for someone this is not necessary he must abandon it. There are no rigid rules. Today when I spoke to one of the participants I explained that for her there were other elements which should be accentuated, but I speak now in general, for the majority, because most people have exactly this type of obstacle.

Let's now take plastic exercises. Since plastic exercises are ultimately a reassembling of stereotyped details, you should always seek a concrete reaction, that is to say bring yourself near to concrete action. For example, caress a woman and destroy all that is stereotyped. Obviously everyone must do this in his own fashion. It must be properly understood that if you do it with calculated thought it will not give the desired result. For instance, you take some paper and start to write: "What will the dialogue be between my left foot and my right foot?" This is stupid. It will not give results since you have spoken with your mind and not with your foot which has a language of its own.

Next I want to give you some advice: do not concentrate too much on problems which in most theatres are ultimately those of the director and not the actor. In certain special theatres which want to bypass barriers, these are already the problems of the actor. But in the theatres in which you will probably work it is different.

Above all, do not now think that make-up is bad and therefore to be avoided. Think how you can transform yourself without its help. But if you have to use make-up, do so. If you have really studied the changes possible without make-up, when you use it you will be much more expressive, and you will be able to surpass all technical tricks.

232

Through fixed impulses and reactions, through a score of fixed details, seek what is personal and intimate. Here, one of the great dangers is that you do not act in true accord with the others. In this case, when you are concentrating on the personal element as on a kind of treasure, if you are looking for the richness of your emotions, the result will be a kind of narcissism. If you want to have emotions at all costs, if you want to have a rich "psyche", that is if you artifically stimulate the internal process, you will only imitate emotions. It is a lie both towards the others and towards yourself.

How does it all start?

It always starts with emotions or psychic reactions with which you are not familiar. For example, a character in the play must kill his mother – but have you in real life killed your mother? No. But maybe you have killed someone. If so, all is well as you will be able to draw on the experience, but if you have not killed you must not search for the feelings or ask yourself what is the psychic state of a man who has killed his mother. It is impossible for you as you have no experience of such an act. But perhaps you once killed an animal. Perhaps this was a powerful experience for you. How did you see the animal? How were your hands behaving? Were you concentrating or not? Did you do it willingly or was there an internal struggle? For example, you ought not to do it but it would be fun to do. Finally in the play where you must kill your mother you can do it by going back to your feelings when you killed a cat, and it will be a cruel analysis of the situation because the acting will not be grandiose and tragic but will only display a small personal obsession. Furthermore, returning to the memory of having killed a cat when you have to kill your mother is not banal.

But if you have to act in a scene where you have to kill an animal, the concrete memory of what it was like when you actually killed an animal is not enough – you must find a reality which is more difficult for you. It is not difficult for you to show you were cruel then – i. e. very dramatic. Thus it is no sacrifice for you. Find something more intimate. For example, do you think that the fact of killing an animal in this scene should give you a thrill, a sort of climax? Perhaps you answer yes, and if you want to say yes, seek in your own memories moments of intense physical climax which are too precious to be shared with others. It is on this memory that you must draw at the time of killing the animal in the play, this concrete memory, so intimate, so little meant for the eyes of others that it will not be easy for you. But if you do this in reality, if you come back to this memory, it will not be possible for you to tense yourself and be dramatic. The shock of sincerity will be too strong. You will be disarmed and relaxed in front of a task which is too much for you, in front of a task which nearly crushes you. If you do that it will be a great moment, and this is what I mean when I say that by means of concrete details it is possible to attain what is personal. When you achieve this you will be pure, you will be purged, you will be without sin. If the memory is one of sin, after-wards you will be free of this sin. It is a kind of redemption.

Next I want to advise you never in the performance to seek for spontaneity without a score. In the exercises it is a different thing altogether. During a performance no real spontaneity is possible without a score. It would only be an imitation of spon-taneity since you would destroy your spontaneity by chaos. During the exercises the score consists of fixed details and I would advise you (except in very specific improvisations proposed by your director or teacher) to improvise only within this frame-work of details. That is to say, you must know the details of an exercise. Today I want to have the detail thus or thus. I will create these details and you can try to find their different variations and justifications. This will give you an authentic improvisation – other-wise you will be building without foundations. When playing the role, the score is no longer one of details but of signs.

I do not wish to explain now what a sign is. Ultimately it is a human reaction, purified of all fragments, of all other details which are not of paramount importance. The sign is the clear impulse, the pure impulse. The actions of the actors are for us signs. If you want a clear definition, it is what I have said earlier: when I do not perceive, it means there are no signs. I said when I "perceive" and not when I "understand", because to understand is a function of the brain. Often we can see, during the play, things we do not understand but which we perceive and feel. In other words, I know what it is I feel. I cannot define it but I know what it is. It is nothing to do with the mind; it affects other associations, other parts of the body. But if I perceive, it means that there was a sign. The test of a true impulse is whether I believe in it or not.

I also want to advise you that if you want to create a true masterpiece, always avoid clichés. Do not follow the easiest road of associations. When you say "What a beautiful day", you must not always say "What a beautiful day" with a happy intonation. When you say "Today I am a little sad", you must not always say it with a sad intonation. That is a cliché, it is commonplace. Man is far more complicated. We hardly ever believe what we say. When a woman says "Today I am sad", what is she really thinking? Perhaps she wanted to say "Go away" or else "I am lonely". You must be conscious of the action behind the words. For example, when using the word "beautiful" I speak with joy in my voice. Almost always the deeper meaning of our reaction is hidden. You must know what the authentic reaction conveyed by the words really is and not illustrate the words alone.

When a man says a prayer he has different reactions, different impulses and different motives. Perhaps he is seeking help or giving thanks. Maybe he wants to forget something unpleasant. Words are always pretexts. Words must never be illustrated. It is the same thing with actions. You know, for example, that in a certain scene in a realist play (I consciously take the example of the realist play for all I have said can also be applied to the realist repertoire) there are times when you are supposed to be bored. Everything must be boring for you. What does the bad actor do in this case? He illustrates the action; his gestures and movements imitate his representation of a man being bored. But to be bored really is to try to find something capable of interesting you. A man in this situation is very active. He may start by reading a book, but this book does not keep his interest. Then he wants something to eat. But everything tastes bad today. Then he wants to go and see something in the garden, but today the garden is not attractive, the air is foul, the atmosphere depressing. So he tries to sleep. That too is concrete. But today sleep eludes him. In other words he is always active. He has not the time to play a man who is bored. He acts far more than in other situations. This is the example given by Stanislavski. However, it is also in accordance with the theatre of realism since, when a man does something concrete, when for example he does something for others, when he works and carries out his duties, within these actions there are personal reactions which do not correspond with what he does, with the external idea of his actions.

Another example: an actor has to write an exercise. But in reality, through writing each one of us realizes a different project. One man wants to get it done in order to have time for something else which he considers more important. Another does not like it; he doesn't like his pencil, or his paper; everything is wrong. Another wants to be a good pupil. He wants to show how well he can do his exercise: "The other children have blunt pencils, but I have sharpened mine. The others have torn, dirty papers, but my paper is clean. The others write without really thinking but I, I concentrate hard." This is reality.

So always avoid banality. That is, avoid illustrating the author's words and remarks. **If you want to create a true masterpiece you must always avoid beautiful lies:** the truths on the calender where under each date you find a proverb or saying such as: "He who is good to others will be happy." But this is not true. It is a lie. The spectator, perhaps, is content. The spectator likes easy truths. But we are not there to please or pander to the spectator. We are there to tell the truth.

Let us take, for example, the Madonna. I was speaking to one of the participants, a lady from Finland, and she gave me an example which illustrates this point. She says that when playing the Madonna, whether in a religious or non-religious play, and whether it is a question of the Virgin Mary or simply of motherhood, this blessed motherhood is always played with the mother leaning lovingly over her child. "But" she said "I am a mother and I know that motherhood is at the same time Madonna and cow. That is the real truth." This is not a metaphor, it is true. The mother gives her milk to the child and she has physiological reactions which are not very different to those of a cow. At the same time we can see in motherhood things which are truly holy. Truth is complicated. So, avoid beautiful lies. **Always try to show the unknown side of things to the spectator.** The spectator protests, but afterwards he will not forget what you have done. After a few years the same spectator will say: "He is the one who spoke the truth. He is a great actor."

Always seek for the real truth and not the popular conception of truth. Use your own real, specific and intimate experiences. This means that you must often give the impression of tactlessness. Aim always for authenticity.

At the beginning of this seminar, I gave an example of playing death. You cannot play death as death, for you have no knowledge of death. You can only play your most intimate experience. For instance your experience of love, or your fear when faced with death or suffering. Or else your physiological reaction towards someone who is dead, or a sort of comparison between yourself and the dead person. It is an analytical process. What makes him

237

dead? Now I am limp, I am motionless, but I am alive. Why? Because there is thought. In short, always do what is most intimately linked to your own experience.

I have said here several times that the actor must unveil himself, that he must release that which is most personal and always do it authentically. It is a sort of excess for the spectator. But you should not strive for this. Only act with your whole self. In the most important moment in your role, reveal your most personal and closely guarded experience. At other moments only use signs, but justify those signs. That is enough. You need not come with all this right from the beginning. Proceed step by step, but without falseness, without imitating actions, always with all your personality, all your body. As a result, you will find some day that your body has started to react totally, that is to say it is almost anihilated, it no longer exists. It offers no further resistance. Your impulses are free.

Finally, something which is very important, something which is, in fact, the core of our work: morality. Understand that I am not speaking of morality in the usual, everyday sense. For example, if you have killed someone it is your ethical problem. It is not my affair any more than that of your collaborator, your director. To my eyes, morality, then, is to express in your work the whole truth. It is difficult but it is possible. And it is this which creates all that is great in art. Certainly it is much easier to speak of the experience of killing someone. There is pathos in that. But there are other much more personal problems which do not have the great pathos of crime, and to have the courage to speak of these is to create greatness in art.

I have repeated here several times, because I think it essential, that you must be strict in your work and you must be well organized and disciplined, and the fact that the work is tiring is absolutely necessary. Often you must be totally exhausted in order to break down the mind's resistance and begin to act with truth.

95.

95-96. **Kordian.** Scenic arrangement. The action takes place in a mental hospital, the spectators being treated as patients. Kordian's actions **(Z. Cynkutis)** are considered as symptoms of his madness. While believing himself to be on the top of Mont Blanc (photo 96), solemnly offering his blood for his country, in reality he is being bled and thus cured of his sick dreams **(Z. Cynkutis, Z. Molik, A. Jaholkowski). Photo: Weglowski.**

96.

97. **Kordian:** The doctor treats one of his patients, surrounded by spectators. **Photo: Weglowski.**

However, I do not mean that you have to be a masochist. When it is necessary, when your director has given you a task, when the rehearsal is in progress – at these moments you must be un-bound by time and fatigue. The rules of work are hard. There is no place here for mimosa, untouchable in its fragility. But do not always seek sad associations of suffering, of cruelty. Seek also the bright and luminous. Often we can be opened by sensual recollections of beautiful days, by memories of paradise lost, by the memory of moments, short in themselves, when we were truly opened, when we had confidence, when we were happy. This is often more difficult than to penetrate into the dark stretches, since it is a treasure we do not wish to give. But often this brings the possibility of finding confidence in one's work, a relaxation which is not technical but which is founded on the right impulse.

When I speak, for example, of the necessity for silence during work, I speak of something which is difficult from a practical point of view, but which is absolutely necessary. Without outward silence you cannot achieve inward silence, the silence of the mind. When you want to reveal your treasure, your sources, then you must work in silence. Avoid all elements of private life, pri-vate contact, whispering, talking, etc. You can enjoy yourself while working but within the bounds of the work and not in a private fashion. Otherwise you will not achieve good results.

After this I want to tell you that you will not reach great heights if you orientate yourself towards the public. I am not speaking of direct contact, but of a type of bondage, the desire to be acclaimed, to win applause and words of esteem. It is impossible, working thus, to create something great. Great works are always sources of conflict. True artists do not have an easy life and are not, to begin with, acclaimed and carried shoulder high. At the start and for a long time, there is a hard struggle. The artist speaks the truth. This truth is nearly always different from the popular conception of truth. The public does not like to be taxed by problems. It is much easier for the spectator to find in the play what he already knows. So, there is a conflict. But afterwards, step by step, the same public begins to realize that it is these same artists, these peculiar artists, whom they cannot forget. Then there is a moment when you could be said to have achieved glory. And you have earned the right to speak the truths which are not popular ones. At that moment there are two possibilities. Either you have found that this social position is very important to you and this means you have blocked all possible further development. You are already frightened of losing your position so you only say the same things the others say. Or you still feel free as an artist. You are not yet orientated towards the public. You always seek the truth, even that which is hidden deepest. Then you will go further and will remain a great man.

In Poland, before the war, there was a renowned actor who found an excellent word for this orientation towards the public. Plants reach towards the sun. In this context we talk of tropism. So this actor, Osterwa, spoke of "publicotropism". This is the actor's worst enemy.

American Encounter

This interview is a fragment of a more extensive one conducted on December 1, 1967, in New York. Jerzy Grotowski, together with his collaborator Ryszard Cieslak, had just completed a four-week course for some students at New York University's School of the Arts. Present at the interview were Theodore Hoffman, Richard Schechner, Jacques Chwat and Mary Tierney. Jacques Chwat served as Jerzy Grotowski's interpreter both during the course and the interview. The complete text of the interview has been published in **The Drama Review,** TDR (Volume 13, No. 1, Fall, 1968).

SCHECHNER: You often talk about the "artistic ethic", what it means to live the artistic life.

GROTOWSKI: During the course I did not use the word "ethic", but nevertheless at the heart of what I said there was an ethical attitude. Why didn't I use the word "ethic"? People who talk about ethics usually want to impose a certain kind of hypocrisy on others, a system of gestures and behavior that serves as an ethic. Jesus Christ suggested ethical duties, but despite the fact that he had miracles at his disposal, he did not succeed in improving mankind. Then why renew this effort?

Perhaps we should ask ourselves only which actions get in the way of artistic creativity. For example, if during creation we hide the things that function in our personal lives, you may be sure that our creativity will fall. We present an unreal image of ourselves; we do not express ourselves and we begin a kind of intellectual or philosophical flirtation – we use tricks and creativity is impossible.

We cannot hide our personal, essential things – even if they are sins. On the contrary, if these sins are very deeply rooted –

perhaps not even sins, but temptations – we must open the door to the cycle of associations. The creative process consists, however, in not only revealing ourselves, but in structuring what is revealed. If we reveal ourselves with all these temptations, we transcend them, we master them through our consciousness.

That is really the kernel of the ethical problem: do not hide that which is basic, it makes no difference whether the material is moral or immoral; our first obligation in art is to express ourselves through our own most personal motives.

Another thing which is part of the creative ethic is taking risks. In order to create one must, each time, take all the risks of failure. That means we cannot repeat an old or familiar route. The first time we take a route there is a penetration into the unknown, a solemn process of searching, studying, and confronting which evokes a special "radiation" resulting from contradiction. This contradiction consists of mastering the unknown – which is nothing other than a lack of self-knowledge – and finding the techniques for forming, structuring, and recognizing it. The process of getting self-knowledge gives strength to one's work.

The second time we come to the same material, if we take the old route we no longer have this unknown within us to refer to; only tricks are left – stereotypes that may be philosophical, moral, or technical. You see, it's not an ethical question. I'm not talking about the "great values". Self-research is simply the right of our profession, our first duty. You may call it ethical, but personally I prefer to treat it as part of the technique because that way there is no sense of its being sweet or hypocritical.

The third thing one could consider "ethical" is the problem of process and result. When I work – either during a course or while directing – what I say is never an objective truth. Whatever I say are stimuli which give the actor a chance to be creative. I say, "fix your attention on this", search for this solemn and recogni-

zable process. You must not think of the result. But, at the same
time, finally, you can't ignore the result because from the objective
point of view the deciding factor in art is the result. In that way,
art is immoral. He is right who has the result. That's the way it is.
But in order to get the result – and this is the paradox – you must
not look for it. If you look for it you will block the natural creative
process. In looking only the brain works; the mind imposes solutions it already knows and you begin juggling known things. That
is why we must look without fixing our attention on the result.
What do we look for? What, for example, are my associations, my
key memories – recognizing these not in thought but through my
body's impulses; to become conscious of them, mastering and
organizing them, and finding out whether they are stronger now
than when they were unformed. Do they reveal more to us or
less? If less, then we have not structured them well.

One must not think of the result and the result will come; there
will be a moment when the fight for the result will be fully
conscious and inevitable, engaging our entire mental machinery.
The only problem is when.

It is the moment when our living creative material is concretely
present. At that point one can use one's mind to structure the
associations and to study the relationship with the audience.
Things which were prohibited earlier are inevitable here. And, of
course, there are individual variations. There is the possibility that
someone will begin with the play of the mind and then later leave
it for a time and still later come back to it. If this is your way, still
do not think of the result but of the process of recognizing the
living material.

Another problem called "ethics". If one formulates what I am
about to formulate, one thinks of it as being very ethical; but I
have found at the base of it a completely objective and technical
problem. The principle is that the actor, in order to fulfil himself,
must not work for himself. Through penetrating his relationship

with others – studying the elements of contact – the actor will discover what is in him. He must give himself totally.

But there is a problem. The actor has two possibilities. Either (1) he plays for the audience – which is completely natural if we think of the theatre's function – which leads him to a kind of flirtation that means that he is playing for himself, for the satisfaction of being accepted, loved, affirmed – and the result is narcissism; or (2) he works directly for himself. That means he observes his emotions, looks for the richness of his psychic states – and this is the shortest way to hypocrisy and hysteria. Why hypocrisy? Because all psychic states observed are no longer lived because emotion observed is no longer emotion. And there is always the pressure to pump up great emotions within oneself. But emotions do not depend upon our wills. We begin to imitate emotions within ourselves, and that is pure hypocrisy. Then the actor looks for something concrete in himself and the easiest thing is hysteria. He hides within hysterical reactions: formless improvisations with wild gestures and screams. This, too, is narcissism. But if acting is not for the audience and not for oneself, what is left?

The answer is a difficult one. One begins by finding those scenes that give the actor a chance to research his relationship with others. He penetrates the elements of contact in the body. He concretely searches for those memories and associations which have decisively conditioned the form of contact. He must give himself totally to this research. In that sense it is like authentic love, deep love. But there is no answer to the question, "love for whom?" Not for God who no longer functions for our generation. And not for nature or pantheism. These are smoky mysteries. Man always needs another human being who can absolutely fulfil and understand him. But that is like loving the Absolute or the Ideal, loving someone who understands you but whom you've never met.

Someone you are searching for. There is no single, simple answer.

One thing is clear: the actor must give himself and not play for himself or for the spectator. His search must be directed from within himself **to** the outside, but not **for** the outside.

When the actor begins to work through contact, when he begins to live in relation to someone – not his stage partner but the partner of his own biography – when he begins to penetrate through a study of his body's impulses, the relationship of this contact, this process of exchange, there is always a rebirth in the actor. Afterwards he begins to use the other actors as screens for his life's partner, he begins to project things on to the characters in the play. And this is his second rebirth.

Finally the actor discovers what I call the "secure partner", this special being in front of whom he does everything, in front of whom he plays with the other characters and to whom he reveals his most personal problems and experiences. This human being – this "secure partner" – cannot be defined. But at the moment when the actor discovers his "secure partner" the third and strongest rebirth occurs, a visible change in the actor's behavior. It is during this third rebirth that the actor finds solutions to the most difficult problems: how to create while one is controlled by others, how to create without the security of creation, how to find a security which is inevitable if we want to express **ourselves** despite the fact that theatre is a **collective** creation in which we are controlled by many people and working during hours that are imposed on us.

One need not define this "secure partner" to the actor, one need only say "you must give yourself absolutely" and many actors understand. Each actor has his own chance of making this discovery, and it's a completely different chance for each. This third rebirth is neither for oneself nor for the spectator. It is most paradoxical. It gives the actor his greatest range of possibilities. One can think of it as ethical, but truly it is technical – despite the fact that it is also mysterious.

SCHECHNER: Two related questions. Several times you told students – particularly during the exercises plastiques (which I will describe later) – to "surpass yourselves", "have courage", "go beyond". And you also said that one must resign oneself "not to do". First question: What is the relationship between surpassing oneself and resigning oneself? Second question – and I ask them together because I feel they are related, though I don't know why: Several times when we were working with scenes from Shakespeare you said, "Don't play the text, you are not Juliet, you didn't write the text". What did you mean?

GROTOWSKI: Without a doubt your questions are related, your impulses are very precise. But it is very difficult to explain. I know what the relationship is but it is difficult for me to express it in logical terms. I accept that. At a certain point, traditional logic does not function. There was a period during my career when I wanted to find the logical explanation for everything. I made formulas that were abstract so that they could encompass two divergent processes. But these abstract formulas were not real; I made pretty sentences which gave the impression that everything was logical. This was cheating, and I decided never again. When I don't know why, I don't try to devise formulas. But often it's a problem of different logical systems. In life we have both formal and paradoxical logic. The paradoxical logical system is strange to our civilization but quite common to oriental or medieval thought. It will be difficult for me to explain the relationship you sensed in your questions, but I think I can explain the consequences of that relationship.

When I say "go beyond yourself" I am asking for an insupportable effort. One is obliged not to stop despite fatigue and to do things that we know well we cannot do. That means one is also obliged to be courageous. What does this lead to? There are certain points of fatigue which break the control of the mind, a control that blocks us. When we find the courage to do things that are

248

impossible, we make the discovery that our body does not block us. We do the impossible and the division within us between conception and the body's ability disappears. This attitude, this determination, is a training for how to go beyond our limits. These are not the limits of our nature, but those of our discomfort. These are the limits we impose upon ourselves that block the creative process, because creativity is never comfortable. If we begin really to work with associations during the **exercises plastiques,** transforming the body movements into a cycle of personal impulses – at that moment we must prolong our determination and not look for the easy. We can "act it" in the bad sense, calculating a move, a look, and thoughts. This is simply pumping.

What will unblock the natural and integral possibilities? To act – that is to react – not to conduct the process but to refer it to personal experiences and to be conducted. The process must take us. At these moments one must be internally passive but externally active. The formula of resigning oneself "not to do" is a stimulus. But if the actor says, "Now I must decide to find my experiences and my intimate associations, I must find my 'secure partner'", he will be very active, but he will be like somebody confessing who has already written everything out in pretty sentences. He confesses, but it's nothing. But if he resigns himself "not to do" this difficult thing and refers himself to things that are truly personal and externalizes these, he would find a very difficult truth. This internal passivity gives the actor the chance to be taken. If one begins too early to conduct the work, then the process is blocked.

SCHECHNER: So that's why you said, "Don't play the text". It wasn't time yet.

GROTOWSKI: Yes. If the actor wants to play the text, he is doing what's easiest. The text has been written, he says it with feeling

249

and he frees himself from the obligation of doing anything himself. But if, as we did during the last days of the course, he works with a silent score – saying the text only in his thoughts – he unmasks this lack of personal action and reaction. Then the actor is obliged to refer to himself within his own context and to find his own line of impulses. One can either not say the text at all or one can "recite" it as a quotation. The actor thinks he is quoting, but he finds the cycle of thought which is revealed in the words. There are many possibilities. In the Desdemona murder scene we worked on in the course her text functioned as erotic love-play. Those words became the actresses' – it didn't matter that she didn't write them. The problem is always the same: stop the cheating, find the authentic impulses. The goal is to find a meeting between the text and the actor.

HOFFMAN: When the students were doing private work you demanded absolute silence. This was hard to get because it runs against our tradition where we are all "sympathetic collaborators" responding with "love" to our fellow actor. A few words on this.

GROTOWSKI: Lack of tact is my specialty. In this country I have observed a certain external friendliness which is part of your daily mask. People are very "friendly", but it is terribly difficult for them to make authentic contact; basically they are very lonely. If we fraternize too easily, without etiquette or ceremony, natural contact is impossible. If you are sincere with another, the other treats that as part of the daily mask.

I find that people here function and behave like instruments or objects. For example – and this has happened to me frequently – I am invited out by people who are not my friends. After a few drinks they begin hysterically to confess themselves and they put me in the position of a judge. It's a role that is imposed on me, as if I were a chair to be sat on. I am as much a judge as a consumer who goes into a store; at the base of it the store is not there for him – he exists for the store.

There are qualities of behavior in every country that one must break through in order to create. Creativity does not mean using our daily masks but rather to make exceptional situations where our daily masks do not function. Take the actor. He works in front of others, he must confess his most personal motives, he must express things he always hides. He must do this consciously, in a structured way, because an inarticulate confession is no confession at all. What blocks him most are his fellow actors and the director. If he listens to the reactions of others he will close himself. He wonders if his confession is funny. He thinks he may become the object of behind-the-back discussion, and he cannot reveal himself. Every actor who privately discusses the intimate associations of another actor knows that when he expresses his own personal motives he, too, will be the subject of someone else's jokes. Thus one must impose on the actors and the director a rigid obligation to be discreet. It's not an ethical problem, but a professional obligation – like those we impose on doctors and lawyers.

Silence is something else. The actor is always tempted into public-tropism. This blocks the deep processes and results in that flirtation I talked about before. For example, an actor does something that one may call funny in the positive sense; his colleagues laugh. Then he begins pumping to make them laugh more. And what was at first a natural reaction becomes artificial.

There is also the problem of creative passivity. It's difficult to express, but the actor must begin by doing nothing. Silence. Full silence. This includes his thoughts. External silence works as a stimulus. If there is absolute silence and if, for several moments, the actor does absolutely nothing, this internal silence begins and it turns his entire nature toward its sources.

SCHECHNER: I would like now to move into a related area. A lot of work in the course and, as I understand it, in your troupe is concerned with the exercises plastiques. I don't want to translate this term because the work is not exactly what we understand in English as "body movement". Your exercises are psycho-physical; there is an absolute unity between the psychical and the physical, the associations of the body are also the associations of the feelings. How did you develop these exercises and how do they function in the training and in the mise en scène?

GROTOWSKI: All the movement exercises had, at first, a completely different function. Their development is the result of a great deal of experimentation. For example, we began by doing yoga directed toward absolute concentration. Is it true, we asked, that yoga can give actors the power of concentration? We observed that despite all our hopes the opposite happened. There was a certain concentration, but it was introverted. This concentration destroys all expression; it's an internal sleep, an inexpressive equilibrium: a great rest which ends all actions. This should have been obvious because the goal of yoga is to stop three processes: thought, breathing, and ejaculation. That means all life processes are stopped and one finds fullness and fulfillment in conscious death, autonomy enclosed in our own kernel. I don't attack it, but it's not for actors.

But we also observed that certain yoga positions help very much the natural reactions of the spinal column; they lead to a sureness of one's body, a natural adaptation to space. So why get rid of them? Just change all their currents. We began to search, to look for different types of contact in these exercises. How could we transform the physical elements into elements of human contact? By playing with one's partner. A living dialogue with the body, with the partner we have evoked in our imagination, or perhaps between the parts of the body where the hand speaks to the leg

252

without putting this dialogue into words or thought. These almost paradoxical positions go beyond the limits of naturalism.

We also began to work with the Delsarte system. I was very interested in Delsarte's thesis that there are introverted and extroverted reactions in human contact. At the same time I found his thesis very stereotyped; it was really very funny as actor training, but there was something to it so I studied it. We began searching through Delsarte's program for those elements which are not stereotyped. Afterwards we had to find new elements of our own in order to realize the goal of our program. Then the personality of the actor working as instructor became instrumental. The physical exercises were largely developed by the actors. I only asked the questions, the actors searched. One question was followed by another. Some of the exercises were conditioned by an actress who had great difficulty with them. For that reason I made her an instructor. She was ambitious and now she is a great master of these exercises – but we searched together.

Later we found that if one treats the exercises as purely physical, an emotive hypocrisy, beautiful gestures with the emotions of a fairy-dance develop. So we gave that up and began to look for personal justification in small details. By playing with colleagues with a sense of surprise, of the unexpected – real justifications which are unexpected – how to fight, how to make unkind gestures, how to parody oneself, and so on. At that moment, the exercises took life.

With these exercises we looked for a conjunction between the structure of an element and the associations which transform it into the mode of each particular actor. How can one conserve the objective elements and still go beyond them toward a purely subjective work? This is the contradiction of acting. It's the kernel of the training.

There are different kinds of exercises. The program is always open. When we are working on a production we do not use the exercises in a play. If we did, it would be stereotyped. But for certain plays, certain scenes, we may have to do special exercises. Sometimes something is left from these for the basic program.

There have been periods – up to eight months – when we have done no exercises at all. We found that we were doing the exercises for their own sake and we gave them up. The actors began to approach perfection, they did impossible things. It was like the tiger who ate his own tail. At that point we stopped the exercises for eight months. When we resumed them they were completely different. The body developed new resistances, the people were the same but they had changed. And we resumed with a great deal more personalization.

Statement of Principles

Jerzy Grotowski wrote this text for internal use within his Theatre Laboratory, and in particular for those actors undergoing a period of trial before being accepted into the troupe in order to acquaint them with the basic principles inspiring the work.
Translation: Maja Buszewicz and Judy Barba.

I

The rhythm of life in modern civilisation is characterised by pace, tension, a feeling of doom, the wish to hide our personal motives and the assumption of a variety of roles and masks in life (different ones with our family, at work, amongst friends or in community life, etc.). We like to be "scientific", by which we mean discursive and cerebral, since this attitude is dictated by the course of civilisation. But we also want to pay tribute to our biological selves, to what we might call physiological pleasures. We do not want to be restricted in this sphere. Therefore we play a double game of intellect and instinct, thought and emotion; we try to divide ourselves artificially into body and soul. When we try to liberate ourselves from it all we start to shout and stamp, we convulse to the rhythm of music. In our search for liberation we reach biological chaos. We suffer most from a lack of totality, throwing ourselves away, squandering ourselves.

Theatre – through the actor's technique, his art in which the living organism strives for higher motives – provides an opportunity for what could be called integration, the discarding of masks, the revealing of the real substance: a totality of physical and mental

255

reactions. This opportunity must be treated in a disciplined manner, with a full awareness of the responsibilities it involves. Here we can see the theatre's therapeutic function for people in our present day civilisation. It is true that the actor accomplishes this act, but he can only do so through an encounter with the spectator – intimately, visibly, not hiding behind a cameraman, wardrobe mistress, stage designer or make-up girl – in direct confrontation with him, and somehow "instead of" him. The actor's act – discarding half measures, revealing, opening up, emerging from himself as opposed to closing up – is an invitation to the spectator. This act could be compared to an act of the most deeply rooted, genuine love between two human beings – this is just a comparison since we can only refer to this "emergence from oneself" through analogy. This act, paradoxical and borderline, we call a total act. In our opinion it epitomizes the actor's deepest calling.

II

Why do we sacrifice so much energy to our art? Not in order to teach others but to learn with them what our existence, our organism, our personal and unrepeatable experience have to give us; to learn to break down the barriers which surround us and to free ourselves from the breaks which hold us back, from the lies about ourselves which we manufacture daily for ourselves and for others; to destroy the limitations caused by our ignorance and lack of courage; in short, to fill the emptiness in us: to fulfil ourselves. Art is neither a state of the soul (in the sense of some extraordinary, unpredictable moment of inspiration) nor a state of man (in the sense of a profession or social function). Art is a ripening, an evolution, an uplifting which enables us to emerge from darkness into a blaze of light.

We fight then to discover, to experience the truth about ourselves; to tear away the masks behind which we hide daily. We see theatre – especially in its palpable, carnal aspect – as a place of provocation, a challenge the actor sets himself and also, indirectly, other people. Theatre only has a meaning if it allows us to transcend our stereotyped vision, our conventional feelings and customs, our standards of judgement – not just for the sake of doing so, but so that we may experience what is real and, having already given up all daily escapes and pretences, in a state of complete defenselessness unveil, give, discover ourselves. In this way – through shock, through the shudder which causes us to drop our daily masks and mannerisms – we are able, without hiding anything, to entrust ourselves to something we cannot name but in which live Eros and Charitas.

III

Art cannot be bound by the laws of common morality or any chatechism. The actor, at least in part, is creator, model and creation rolled into one. He must not be shameless as that leads to exhibitionism. He must have courage, but not merely the courage to exhibit himself – a passive courage, we might say: the courage of the defenseless, the courage to reveal himself. Neither that which touches the interior sphere, nor the profound stripping bare of the self should be regarded as evil so long as in the process of preparation or in the completed work they produce an act of creation. If they do not come easily and if they are not signs of outburst but of mastership, then they are creative: they reveal and purify us **while we transcend ourselves.** Indeed, they improve us then.

For these reasons every aspect of an actor's work dealing with intimate matters should be protected from incidental remarks, indiscretions, nonchalance, idle comments and jokes. The personal realm – both spiritual and physical – must not be "swamped" by triviality, the sordidness of life and lack of tact towards oneself and others; at least not in the place of work or anywhere connected with it. This postulate sounds like an abstract moral order. It is not. It involves the very essence of the actor's calling. This calling is realized through carnality. The actor must not **illustrate** but **accomplish** an "act of the soul" by means of his own organism. Thus he is faced with two extreme alternatives: he can either sell,

257

dishonour, his real "incarnate" self, making himself an object of artistic prostitution; or he can give himself, sanctify his real "incarnate" self.

IV

An actor can only be guided and inspired by someone who is whole-hearted in his creative activity. The producer, while guiding and inspiring the actor, must at the same time allow himself to be guided and inspired by him. It is a question of freedom, partnership, and this does not imply a lack of discipline but a respect for the autonomy of others. Respect for the actor's autonomy does not mean lawlessness, lack of demands, never ending discussions and the replacement of action by continuous streams of words. On the contrary, respect for autonomy means enormous demands, the expectation of a maximum creative effort and the most personal revelation. Understood thus, sollicitude for the actor's freedom can only be born from the plenitude of the guide and not from his lack of plenitude. Such a lack implies imposition, dictatorship, superficial dressage.

V

An act of creation has nothing to do with either external comfort or conventional human civility; that is to say, working conditions in which everybody is happy. It demands a maximum of silence and a minimum of words. In this kind of creativity we discuss through proposals, actions and living organisms, not through explanations. When we finally find ourselves on the track of something difficult and often almost intangible, we have no right to lose it through frivolity and carelessness. Therefore, even during breaks after which we will be continuing with the creative process, we are obliged to observe certain natural reticences in our behaviour and even in our private affairs. This applies just as much to our own work as to the work of our partners. We must not interrupt and disorganize the work because we are hurrying to our own affairs; we must not peep, comment or make jokes about it privately. In any case, private ideas of fun have no place in the actor's calling. In our approach to creative tasks, even if the theme is a game, we must be in a state of readiness – one might even say "solemnity". Our working terminology which serves as a stimulus must not be dissociated from the work and used in a private context. Work terminology should be associated only with that which it serves.

A creative act of this quality is performed in a group, and therefore within certain limits we should restrain our creative egoism. An actor has no right to mould his partner so as to provide greater possibilities for his own performance. Nor has he the right to correct his partner unless authorized by the work leader. Intimate or drastic elements in the work of others are untouchable and should not be commented upon even in their absence. Private conflicts, quarrels, sentiments, animosities are unavoidable in any human group. It is our duty towards creation to keep them in check in so far as they might deform and wreck the work process. We are obliged to open ourselves up even towards an enemy.

VI

It has been mentioned several times already, but we can never stress and explain too often the fact that we must never exploit privately anything connected with the creative act: i. e. location, costume, props, an element from the acting score, a melodic theme or lines from the text. This rule applies to the smallest detail and there can be no exceptions. We did not make this rule simply to pay tribute to a special artistic devotion. We are not interested in grandeur and noble words, but our awareness and experience tell us that lack of strict adherence to such rules causes the actor's score to become deprived of its psychic motives and "radiance".

VII

Order and harmony in the work of each actor are essential conditions without which a creative act cannot take place. Here we demand consistency. We demand it from the actors who come to the theatre consciously to try themselves out in something extreme, a sort of challenge seeking a total response from every one of us. They come to test themselves in something very definite that reaches beyond the meaning of "theatre" and is more like an act of living and way of existence. This outline probably sounds rather vague. If we try to explain it theoretically, we might say that the theatre and acting are for us a kind of vehicle allowing us to emerge from ourselves, to fulfil ourselves. We could go into this at great length. However, anyone who stays here longer than just the trial period is perfectly aware that what we are talking about can be grasped less through grandiose words than through details, demands and the rigours of work in all its elements. The individual who disturbs the basic elements, who does not for example respect his own and the others' acting score, destroying its structure by shamming or automatic reproduction, is the very one who shakes this undefinable higher motive of our common activity. Seemingly small details form the background against which fundamental questions are decided, as for example the duty to note down elements discovered in the course of the work. We must not rely on our memory unless we feel the spontaneity of our work is being threatened, and even then we must keep a partial record. This is just as basic a rule as is strict punctuality, the thorough memorizing of the text, etc. Any form of shamming in one's work is completely inadmissible. However it does sometimes happen that an actor has to go through a scene, just outline it, in order to check its organization and the elements of his partners' actions. But even then he must follow the actions carefully, measuring himself against them, in order to comprehend their motives. This is the difference between outlining and shamming.

An actor must always be ready to join the creative act at the exact moment determined by the group. In this respect his health, physical condition and all his private affairs cease to be just his own concern. A creative act of such quality flourishes only if nourished by the living organism. Therefore we are obliged to take daily care of our bodies so we are always ready for our tasks.

We must not go short of sleep for the sake of private enjoyment and then come to work tired or with a hangover. We must not come unable to concentrate. The rule here is not just one's compulsory presence in the place of work, but physical readiness to create.

VIII

Creativity, especially where acting is concerned, is boundless sincerity, yet disciplined: i. e. articulated through signs. The creator should not therefore find his material a barrier in this respect. And as the actor's material is his own body, it should be trained to obey, to be pliable, to respond passively to psychic impulses as if it did not exist during the moment of creation – by which we mean it does not offer any resistance. Spontaneity and discipline are the basic aspects of an actor's work and they require a methodical key.

Before a man decides to do something he must first work out a point of orientation and then act accordingly and in a coherent manner. This point of orientation should be quite evident to him, the result of natural convictions, prior observations and experiences in life. The basic foundations of this method constitute for our troupe this point of orientation. Our institute is geared to examining the consequences of this point of orientation. Therefore nobody who comes and stays here can claim a lack of knowledge of the troupe's methodical programme. Anyone who comes and works here and then wants to keep his distance (as regards creative consciousness) shows the wrong kind of care for his own individuality. The etymological meaning of "individuality" is "indivisibility" which means complete existence in something: individuality is the very opposite of half-heartedness. We maintain, therefore, that those who come and stay here discover in our method something deeply related to them, prepared by their lives and experiences. Since they accept this consciously, we presume that each of the participants feels obliged to train creatively and try to form his own variation inseparable from him-

261

self, his own reorientation open to risks and search. For what we here call "the method" is the very opposite of any sort of prescription.

IX

The main point then is that an actor should not try to acquire any kind of recipe or build up a "box of tricks". This is no place for collecting all sorts of means of expression. The force of gravity in our work pushes the actor towards an interior ripening which expresses itself through a willingness to break through barriers, to search for a "summit", for totality.

The actor's first duty is to grasp the fact that nobody here wants **to give** him anything; instead they plan **to take** a lot from him, to take away that to which he is usually very attached: his resistance, reticence, his inclination to hide behind masks, his half-heartedness, the obstacles his body places in the way of his creative act, his habits and even his usual "good manners".

X

Before an actor is able to achieve a total act he has to fulfil a number of requirements, some of which are so subtle, so intangible, as to be practically undefinable through words. They only become plain through practical application. It is easier, however, to define conditions under which a total act cannot be achieved and which of the actor's actions make it impossible.

This act cannot exist if the actor is more concerned with charm, personal success, applause and salary than with creation as understood in its highest form. It cannot exist if the actor conditions it according to the size of his part, his place in the performance, the day or kind of audience. There can be no total act if the actor, even away from the theatre, dissipates his creative impulse and, as we said before, sullies it, blocks it, particularly through incidental engagements of a doubtful nature or by the premeditated use of the creative act as a means to further his own career.

262